W9-CZT-344

Formative Assessment in the Age of Accountability

In today's world, schools are being held accountable for student performance on state tests. Summative assessments of this kind provide useful information to the public and to policymakers. But the information they provide is of limited use to teachers, primarily because state assessment results arrive too late to effectively inform instruction. In this book we hope to help teachers develop an informed perspective about formative assessment and how that kind of assessment is an effective tool for instruction that fosters student learning.

There are clear differences between formative and summative assessments. Summative assessments sum up learning. They evaluate student performances in terms of where students are expected to be at the end of an instructional year or grading period.

Formative assessments, on the other hand, are intended to provide feedback and to guide instruction. Teachers who conduct formative assessments gather information about what their students know and are able to do at various points in time; using this information, they make decisions about what students need help with next. They also use this information to provide feedback to students. The best formative assessments, according to Paul Black and his colleagues, are those that provide effective feedback (see, for example, Black & Wiliam, 1998). Black describes the characteristics of such feedback as follows: First, effective feedback must be intelligible so that students can grasp its significance and use it both as a self-assessment tool and as a guide for improvement. Second, effective feedback must focus on particular qualities of the student's work. Third, effective feedback must provide advice about how to improve the work and set an achievable target. To these criteria we would add two caveats: First, effective feedback must evolve as students acquire new skills. Second,

effective feedback about writing should not be generic; it should refer to particular genres and the elements and strategies associated with them.

Learning About Genres

A genre is a rough template for accomplishing a particular purpose with language. It provides the writer and the reader with a common set of assumptions about what characterizes the text. So, for example, if the text is labeled a mystery story, there is an assumption that the story line will be built around some puzzle to be resolved or some crime to be solved. Likewise, when a piece starts off "Once upon a time…," there is an assumption that we will be reading or writing a fairy tale or a parody of a fairy tale. But if the first line of a text is "Whales are mammals," we expect a very different genre—a report of information instead of a story.

As Charles Cooper (1999) explains, writers shape texts to accomplish different purposes by using and adapting particular patterns of organization, by using particular techniques to develop the text, and by making particular language choices. Although there is a lot of variation from one text to another within the same genre, texts in a particular genre nevertheless follow a general pattern. As a result, readers develop expectations that enable them to anticipate where a text is going so they can make sense of it as they read. Writers know how to order and present thoughts in language patterns readers can recognize and follow.

Lack of genre knowledge will impair a student's academic success. The student who is required to produce a report but who does not know the expectations relative to report writing is immediately disadvantaged. That student must guess at how information might be ordered, what kind of stance/persona could be effective, how much information should be provided, and what level of specificity would be sufficient. By comparison, the student who is genre savvy and is aware of the various expectations attached to informational writing can choose which genre expectations to guide his or her writing, which to disregard, and if or where to vary the conventional pattern. This genre-savvy student enjoys a tremendous advantage over the first student.

Genre knowledge also supports reading comprehension. If children are familiar with the structure of a text, they can make predictions and understand the functions of text features such as dialogue, and so read more purposefully. Moreover, being familiar with the text structure also makes it easier for readers to internalize the information in a text. Students who understand the organizational pattern of a text can use this knowledge to locate key information, identify what is important and unimportant, synthesize information that appears in different locations within a text, and organize the information in memory. In general, making readers more aware of genre structure appears to improve comprehension, memory, and, thus, learning.

Several genres are fundamental to writing development in kindergarten through fifth grade. The four that are discussed in this book and the others in the grade-by-grade New Standards rubrics series are (1) narrative writing (sharing events, telling stories), (2) report of information (informing others), (3) instructions (instructing others about how to get things done), and (4) responding to literature. The characteristic features of each of these genres are presented in rubrics that describe different levels of performance.

In their current form, the rubrics in this book are not designed to be used with students. They are too complex, and their language is too abstract for children. However, the rubrics can easily serve as templates for guiding the development of grade-level-appropriate classroom rubrics that address elements and strategies. They are, in effect, end-of-the-year targets from which a teacher maps backward to plan instruction.

What Makes a Rubric Good to Use With Students?

Rubrics can be developed and used in formative or summative ways. Typically, rubrics used in summative evaluation are short. They provide a minimum amount of detail so that scorers can quickly and efficiently assign a score to a piece of student writing. Rubrics used in summative assessment are also static, out of necessity. After all, only by using the same rubric can you get comparative data in order to report trends over time. Further, they represent how students are expected to write at the end of a grading period. Summative rubrics don't provide information about the road along the way. Formative rubrics, on the other hand, trace patterns of development and focus on the particular.

Focus on the Particular

The brevity required for efficient scoring and the static nature of summative rubrics fight against what teachers and students need to foster writing development. For example, it is not enough for a writer to be told that his or her writing is "well organized," a phrase commonly found on generic rubrics in state assessments. Such a global statement does not help the writer understand what it takes to make writing well organized. A more effective descriptor would be, "Clearly sequences events in the story and maintains control of point of view."

Be Intelligible

Formative rubrics must also be meaningful to students. Ideally, they should grow out of the work of the classroom and represent a consensus about what constitutes good writing. They must be written in language that the students understand, language that is familiar. The goal is for students to be able to self-assess their writing in order to take on productive revisions and interact with peers in response groups or with the teacher in a conference. The language of the rubric should frame such interactions so that they are meaningful to everyone and grounded in the classroom culture.

Set Targets and Offer Advice

Formative rubrics should set targets and offer advice. At each score level, a good rubric provides a list of criteria that defines performance at that level. Advancement to the next level (the target) comes about by refining the paper to match the criteria in the next score level. So, for example, if a student's paper is at score point 3 and that student wants a score point 4, the student must revise the paper to include all the elements for the higher score currently missing from the paper or must refine the way in which the elements and strategies in his or her paper are developed. Rubrics are not good tools for revision if the distinctions between score levels are set only by qualifiers such as "scant" detail, "some" detail, "adequate" detail, and "effective" detail. Better rubrics provide more definitive distinctions such as "no introduction," "an introduction that names the topic and provides at least minimal context," or "an introduction that names the topic, provides context, and generates reader interest." Better rubrics focus on the features and components of particular genres (for example, in narrative, character development, plot, dialogue, flashback). Such rubrics provide students and teachers with language to talk about the ways certain texts accomplish particular purposes. The rubrics presented in this book encompass both the genre elements and the strategies associated with each genre.

Be Developed in a Classroom Setting

Students and teachers need formative rubrics that emerge from the teaching in a classroom and that specify work yet to be done. To learn about genres, students need to be engaged in active inquiry. Guided by their teachers, they can analyze texts of a published author, a peer, or their own work, and develop classroom rubrics as they examine the texts. The texts will serve as examples and inspiration. These classroom rubrics should be constructed as guidelines to improve student writing performance.

When rubrics are constructed as guidelines to improve performance, it is possible for a student, working alone or with a teacher, to use a rubric as a checklist—a rough approximation of what is in place and how well wrought these elements are. Once that is done, the student should be able to study the criteria at the next level to determine what further

Information Writing

	4	3	2	1
Organization	All information is organized logically by headings or chapter titles.	Information is organized but not always logically.	Information is only partly organized.	Information is just a list of facts.
Facts and Details	Lots of facts with concrete detail.	Some facts and details.	A few facts and details.	Just facts with no detail
Graphics	Uses pictures or graphs to paint a picture in reader's mind	Some pictures or graphs.	A few pictures or graphs.	No pictures or graphs.
Beginning Middle End	Has very clear beg–mid–end.	Has beg–mid–end.	Has beg.+mid. but no end.	No beg–mid–end

The above is an example of a classroom rubric, constructed jointly by a teacher and her students. This joint construction ensures a shared understanding about what constitutes good writing and about what "next steps" should guide instruction.

work would need to be done for the writing to show significant improvement.

In some cases, such as when papers are almost at standard, a simple revision by the student is enough to sufficiently improve the quality of the work. The revision conference would have the teacher providing a reminder, such as, "Did you forget x?" or a suggestion, "Why not flesh out your central character's motivation a bit?" No instruction would be necessary; the writer would just need to be nudged a bit. But in other cases, to bring the paper "up to standard" would require significantly more than a nudge. Many papers signal a substantial need for instruction, time, and practice.

Note: Implicit here are two assumptions. One, that it is the job of the teacher to enable the writer and not just "fix" the paper. And two, that learning to write takes time. In some cases, learning to use the elements that define the next higher score point might take up to a year!

Change With Instruction

Formative rubrics grow. Thoughtful teachers know that they have to move students from their initial performances in September to more refined performances at the end of the year. The instruction they provide will make this change possible. Consider the kindergarten students who begin school with no awareness of the conventions of print. When asked to write a story, they will likely draw a picture and perhaps include some random letters. After instruction, and with time, these students will begin to produce writing that moves from left to right, and top to bottom. They likely will copy words from word charts and play with phonetic spelling. Initial rubrics should celebrate this growth with criteria aimed at moving students forward one step at a time.

Older students, too, will improve with focused instruction and practice. Consider a beginning of the year third-grade classroom in which a teacher is doing a study on narration. The first rubric might have as few as three elements in order to represent what students initially know:

1. Has a beginning that interests the reader
2. Has a number of events that taken together tell a story
3. Has some sort of closure

The three-element rubric captures the essence of narrative and, hence, is complete. A more fully developed narrative rubric would also have some mention of transitions and probably some mention of detail. So, the rubric could easily grow from three to five descriptors, as the teacher provides the necessary instruction.

Growing a Rubric

Changing the Number of Levels

Just as the number of descriptors in a rubric may grow, so may the number of levels. Assume the teacher begins the year with a rubric that has three levels: meets the standard, "great writing"; approaches the standard, "O.K. writing"; and needs more work, "ready for revision." As fewer students produce work that falls below standard, the bottom distinctions can disappear (literally be removed/cut off/marked out). Then what was once work that "meets the standard" can become "approaching a higher standard." This can be determined by teacher and students collaboratively. Similarly, work that "met the standard" can now become "ready for revision." Growing a rubric like this—constantly reexamining how good work must be to earn the highest distinction—is a powerful way to highlight student *growth* in writing.

Changing the Anchor Papers

In themselves, rubrics leave much room for ambiguity. They can be made more explicit by providing examples of what they describe. These examples are called *anchor* papers. When the words on the rubric remain unchanged, but the paper that illustrates the level of performance they describe changes, the rubric is said to be "recalibrated." An example will help here: Assume that the rubric simply states, "Has a beginning that engages the reader." The paper that initially illustrates that concept may have a simple opening sentence/phrase ("Once upon a time there lived a king" or "On Saturday, I saw light"). If recalibrated, the anchor paper would provide a more complex beginning, for example: a paragraph or longer that sets a plot in motion, an example of dialogue that immediately creates reader interest, a description that is simply riveting (think of the beginning of *Maniac McGee*), or even the resolution of a story told as a flashback.

Understanding These Rubrics

Elements and Strategies

The rubrics in this book are divided into two parts. The first section delineates the elements that are fundamental to the genre, and the second section lays out the strategies writers frequently employ to enhance the genre.

This division of the rubric is intentional. The elements are of critical importance and are foundational to the genre. Until a writer can address the elements with some proficiency, an instructional focus on strategies is misguided. Yet, it is not unusual for instruction to skip from very basic work on introductions and conclusions to an emphasis on lifting the level of language in a piece, most often by inserting metaphors and similes. While figurative language can distinguish a good piece of writing, it cannot compensate for a fundamental lack of development. Think of the compulsories in an Olympic figure skating event. The skater must demonstrate proficiency performing the athletic stunts required by the judges before attempting the more creative dance moves that are also part of his or her repertoire. Genres, likewise, require the writer to address certain elements.

That is not to say that the strategies are unimportant. Frequently, they work with the elements to carry a reader through the text. Consider the work of dialogue in advancing the plot of a novel. The dialogue provides clues about who characters are and what motivates them. Dialogue also frequently helps a reader make transitions when there are scene changes or shifts in time. But a novel without a well-developed plot, well-developed characters, or some organizational frame will not be made whole simply with the inclusion of dialogue.

Too often, writing instruction in narrative focuses on leads and transitions to structure chronological ordering and on teaching strategies out of context (for instance, including dialogue for the sake of having dialogue, rather than as a strategy to develop character or advance the action). In many classrooms, not enough time is spent on the elements, the "compulsories" of genres. For this reason, the rubrics have been designed to emphasize both strategies and elements. When teachers use the rubrics to analyze students' strengths and weaknesses in order to plan instruction, they should first focus on the elements section. The strategies can be folded in instructionally as students begin to demonstrate awareness of the elements. In some cases, young writers will likely pick up strategies on their own through their reading and by appropriating text from favorite authors.

Note: The lists of elements and strategies provided in these materials are foundational. They are not meant to be exhaustive or exclusive.

Except at the kindergarten level, the scores for the New Standards rubrics are distributed across five levels:

- Score point 5: Work that exceeds the grade-level standard

- Score point 4: Work that meets the standard
- Score point 3: Work that needs only a conference
- Score point 2: Work that needs instruction
- Score point 1: Work that needs substantial support

Score Point 5

Papers at this score point go well beyond grade-level expectations. What sets score point 5 papers apart is the level of sophistication brought to the text by the writer. Occasionally, this sophistication is reflected in the writer's syntax or vocabulary. Sometimes the sophistication is shown by a nuanced execution of writing strategies. Other times it may simply be the level of development that comes from the writer's deep understanding of the topic or the genre. In all cases, what distinguishes a score point 5 is writing development that goes beyond what the school curriculum has provided that writer. Performance at this level is exceptional, beyond what might be expected even after a year's program of effective instruction. This is not to say that students writing at score point 5 could not benefit from instruction. Even adult professional writers work to hone their craft. There are many strategies that a writer can learn and work to refine, and these should be the basis for the teacher's instructional plan for exceptional writers.

Score Point 4

Papers at this score point illustrate a standards-setting performance. They are a full representation of the genre, though some features may be better executed than others.

Score point 4 papers grow out of good teaching, student effort, and quite likely a genre-specific curriculum. These papers "meet the standard" for what students should be able to accomplish if they receive effective instruction.

Note: The criteria that define score points 5 and 4 are identical. This is intentional. What distinguishes a 5 from a 4 is not the presence or absence of a particular element or strategy. Rather, it is the overall quality of execution and the level of language the writer employs. The writers of score point 5 papers frequently also bring something to the text that may not be provided by instruction—a deep understanding or passion for the topic and the genre.

Score Point 3

Generally, the papers at score point 3 do not meet the standard for one of two reasons: (1) the writer did not include a necessary feature, such as a conclusion, or (2) the execution of a strategy was not well done. In either case, the writer of a paper at score point 3 is otherwise competent and needs only a conference to point out the paper's problem in order to revise it upward to a score point 4. The suggestions for improving the paper should come from the criteria at score point 4.

Score point 3 papers are not unusual with novice writers. Many young writers, for example, produce reports without an introduction because they assume that the title of their piece is sufficient to introduce the topic. Or they may not accommodate their readers by providing sufficient detail or a satisfactory ending. Such writers are completely capable of improving these inadequacies when they are pointed out in a teacher–student conference. It is these papers that represent score point 3. To achieve the target of score point 4, a teacher needs only to point out omissions from the criteria listed at score point 4 or the need for refinement in a revision.

Score Point 2

The student writer of a score point 2 paper needs instruction in order to produce work that is up to standard. A quick read-through of the score point 2 paper makes obvious either that there are gaps in the writer's understanding of the genre features or that the writer simply has insufficient control over the strategy he or she is attempting. The instructional next steps are suggested by criteria at score point 4. However, it is almost certain that student work will pass through some of the inadequacies suggested by score point 3 before the writer can produce work that meets standard. The student producing writing at score point 2 needs instruction and practice with feedback. Deep understanding and resulting proficiency could take several months.

Score Point 1

Papers that receive a score point 1 are representative of a writer who needs substantial support. The student writer at score point 1 may need extensive help developing basic fluency and basic genre knowledge to move toward meeting the standard. The criteria at score point 4 outline a map for the student's development. To move from habitually producing work at a score point 1 to typically producing work at a score point 4 will require much support and time, perhaps as much as a year. Along with the classroom support

from the teacher, students who write papers at score point 1 may require access to other kinds of safety nets, such as special programs, in order to make progress toward meeting the standard.

How to Use These Rubrics

Research, as well as practical experience, demonstrate that within any single classroom the range of performance in writing and in children's knowledge of genres is wide. In any particular grade, some students' papers will look like the work of children in earlier grades, whereas the work of other students will appear more advanced. Even the work of a single child will show great variation from day to day because development does not progress smoothly forward in step-by-step increments. Moreover, skills that appear to be mastered are sometimes thrown into disarray as new skills are acquired.

We also know that students write some genres better than others. Research shows that young children typically have more experience with narrative genres than scientific or poetic genres. Research also shows that children are more successful handling the familiar structure of stories than the less familiar structure of arguments. One explanation for these differences may lie in the instruction about genres children receive, or do not receive, in school. Another explanation may be related to their experiences outside of school. If children have had infrequent exposure to particular genres, they will be less adept at writing and reading them than children who have had frequent exposure.

To use these rubrics, a teacher should first ask each student to produce a piece of writing specific to a particular genre. If the genre is narrative, the teacher might say, "I'd like you to write a story about...." If the genre is informational, the teacher might say, "I'd like you to write a report about...." If the genre is instructional writing, "I'd like you to write a paper explaining how to do something." Or if the genre is response to literature, "I'd like you to read this story/ book/poem and then write a paper that explains what the author is saying." A response to literature by kindergarten students might be phrased as, "I'd like you to listen as I read and then write a response."

Once the student writing is in hand, the teacher should analyze individual performances with the appropriate genre rubric. This analysis will indicate what kinds of instruction are needed for students to gain the knowledge and skills required to produce work in that genre at score point 4 (meets the standard).

Note: Making a judgment about proficiency on the basis of a single sample is always chancy. To have a better sense of a student's proficiency, it is always wise to look at several samples.

It is almost certain that student work will not reflect the same level of proficiency for each element or strategy contained in the rubric. That is, a student writer may establish a strong orientation and context (score point 4), but develop character only weakly (score point 2). The student could make good use of dialogue (score point 4), but provide too few details (score point 2). In fact, most papers produced by novice writers are of this uneven quality.

The point of these rubrics is not to assign an overall score to student work, as one might do in a formal assessment, and certainly not to assign a grade. Rather, it is to highlight for teachers the characteristics of student work at different levels of performance so that appropriate instruction and feedback can be provided. Grading student writing is a necessity for teachers, and it is essential that the grades assigned reflect student performance relative to the genre elements and strategies. Grades can be derived from the classroom rubric. See the sample classroom rubric on page 3.

How to Use the Papers and Commentary

Papers at each score point are representative of what work at that score level might look like. They are concrete examples of what the rubric describes. The commentaries describe the student writing in relation to the rubric. Teachers can use the papers and commentaries to calibrate the levels of performance of their own students. Comparing their students' work with the work in this book will highlight for teachers the various levels of proficiency among their students and facilitate instructional planning. Students in upper-elementary grades can study the papers as models of work that represent either a strong performance for a genre, or work that could be strengthened through revision. Teachers can use the commentaries to scaffold discussion, and working together, teachers and students can construct classroom rubrics. A further use for the papers and commentaries is as the focus for teacher meetings where the goal is to establish a shared understanding of what good writing looks like.

In all cases, the commentaries have been written with the intention of honoring what is in place in the papers. Too often, student assessment focuses entirely on what is missing and what is poorly done. This genre-based approach to writing assumes that writing development is a layered process in which new learning builds over time upon what is already in place. The starting point is always first to identify the paper's strengths. In this manner, writing assessment is a positive, additive process, one that is also transparent and meaningful to students.

At the end of each of the commentaries for papers at score points 3, 2, and 1, there is a set of "next-step" suggestions. For score point 3 papers, the set is titled Possible Conference Topics; at score point 2, Next Steps in Instruction; and at score point 1, Roadmap for Development. These different titles are indicative of the kind and amount of support a student will need to produce work that meets the standard (for instance, a short conference at score point 3 versus extended instruction at score point 2). All of these next-step suggestions are simply that—suggestions. It may well be that other sets of suggestions could also work. However, the suggestions provided were drawn from an analysis of dozens of papers typical of that score point, as well as from an analysis of the particular paper described in the commentary. These suggestions were also derived from the rubric criteria at score point 4.

It should be emphasized that students at score point 2 and score point 1 will not move from these score levels without passing through the next higher score level(s). Writing proficiency takes time and practice. There will be some slow steps forward and some backsliding on the students' part. But these are novice writers, so patience, practice, and coaching should be part of any instructional plan.

This book has been designed with insight into the complexities of teaching writing. It includes student work as models and lists of rubric criteria as scales, two things that, according to George Hillocks (1984), research indicates will improve student writing if used appropriately. This book was drawn from the work of dedicated teachers and hard-working students. (To protect their privacy, names have been removed.) Admittedly, this is only one part of a comprehensive writing program, but it will serve well those teachers who use it to plan for student instruction.

The student papers in this book were chosen from more than 5,000 pieces written by students in many different elementary schools in several different school districts. The papers illustrate the range of abilities and performance of students at different grade levels from kindergarten through fifth grade, as well as ranges within grade levels. In the first year of the project, 3,586 students participated. Their teachers taught author and genre studies, and at the end of the year, the teachers collected portfolios of student writing. The examples in this book are drawn from these students' portfolios.

Narrative

Narrative is the genre most commonly associated with elementary schools. In fact, people assume that narrative, or more specifically, story, is the purview of our youngest students. To a large extent this assumption is logical. Elementary school is filled with story—picture books, show and tell, dramas, and basal readers. Children make sense of their lives and their worlds through story. Jerome Bruner (1985) tells us, "They [young children] are not able to…organize things in terms of cause and effect and relationships, so they turn things into stories, and when they try to make sense of their life they use the storied version of their experience as the basis for further reflection. If they don't catch something in a narrative structure, it does not get remembered very well, and it does not seem to be accessible for further kinds of mulling over."

Narratives have time as their deep structure in which a narrative involves a series of events that can be plotted out on some sort of time line. The time span could be short, a few moments, or long, even across generations.

There are many kinds of narratives (frequently called subgenres): memoirs, biographies, accounts, anecdotes, folktales, recounts, mysteries, autobiographies, etc. Recount is a kind of narrative in which the teller simply retells events for the purpose of informing or entertaining. Anecdotes, on the other hand, generally include some kind of crisis that generates an emotional reaction—frustration, satisfaction, insecurity, etc. Stories, in contrast, exhibit a somewhat different pattern. A complication creates a problem, which then has to be overcome (the resolution). Stories are built of events that are causally linked (the events recounted share a cause–effect relationship). Think for a moment about stories. It is quite easy to say of them, "this happened because this happened, so this happened and that caused this to happen." Narrative accounts, by contrast, are comprised of a series of events that in total may or may not add up to anything significant other than the reader's sense of "this is how things went." It is a matter of "this happened and then this and then this and then this." Folktales take yet another form. Like other genres, different subgenres of narrative can serve different purposes, for example, to entertain or to make a point about what people should do, about how the world should be.

The New Standards expectation for student writers around narrative requires that they be able to craft a narrative account, either fiction or nonfiction, that does the following: establishes a context; creates a point of view; establishes a situation or plot; creates an organizing structure; provides detail to develop the event sequence and characters; uses a range of appropriate strategies, such as dialogue; and provides closure.

Orientation and Context

As it relates to narrative, orienting the reader and providing context usually involves bringing readers into the narrative (situating them somehow in the story line) and engaging them.

There are many ways to do this, of course, but among the most common strategies are

- Introducing a character who is somehow interesting
- Establishing a situation that intrigues or startles a reader
- Situating a reader in a time or place
- Having a narrator speak directly to the reader in order to create empathy or interest

From this initial grounding, writers can begin to develop the event sequence of their narratives.

Plot Development and Organization

The organization of narrative is not necessarily a straightforward chronological ordering of events. Consider just a few variations. Narratives frequently are organized as the simultaneously ongoing, unfolding of events in the lives of multiple persons or fictional characters. The end of such a narrative requires that several or all of these persons' or characters' lives come together. In some narratives, the sequence of events may be altered to create interest, so the writer may use flashbacks and flash-forwards to move the characters around in time or to create a "backstory" of the events leading up to the story. Stories within a story are another commonly used device. Mystery stories often are organized by laying out an initiating event (crime), and then providing a series of clues and several false resolutions before the truth is finally revealed. Newspaper stories traditionally flow from the standard "who, what, where, when, why, how?" of an introductory paragraph. Memoir is organized around a single event or series of events that sum up the essence of who someone is, or was, and what values and heritage shaped that person. Biography and autobiography usually begin with birth and move through early years, adolescent years, and late years of someone's life. The diversity of narrative genres, as well as the myriad ways in which they can be developed, serve to remind us of the various options writers have for communicating with readers.

In general, however, narratives are often organized in such a way that some event precipitates a causally linked series of further events, which in some way is ultimately resolved. Episodes share a relationship to each other and usually are built around a problem and emotional response, an action, and an outcome. Nuanced plotting frequently involves subplots, built through episodes, and shifts in time. The classic plot structures for conflict are man vs. man, man vs. society, man vs. nature, and man vs. self.

Although children and adults may tell complicated narratives, it is important to remember that they also tell simple recounts. Recounts tell what happened, and organization is based on a series of events that all relate to a particular occasion. Children often recount personal narratives about school excursions or particularly memorable events in their lives—their immigration to America, the death of a cherished pet, the birth of a sister, and so on. In recounts, sometimes there is not an initiating event; rather, writers present a bed-to-bed story that retells the mundane events of the day.

Adult writers use a variety of methods to develop event sequences and their settings. They typically develop settings by providing details about place, colors, structures, landscape, and so on. They use several techniques to manage event sequences and time, including flashbacks and flash-forwards, forecasting, and back stories. They sometimes manipulate time by compressing or expanding it, that is, by providing pacing. They use dialogue and interior monologue purposefully to advance the action. During the elementary school years, children are just beginning to master these techniques.

Because narratives are based on events in time, writers also often use linking words that deal with time and the organization of events (then, before, after, when, while). When people recount events, they often refer to the specific times when events happened (yesterday, last summer). As children mature, their repertoire of temporal signals develops, from simple transition words (then, after, before) to more complex phrases ("At the time…") and clauses ("Before he went in the house…").

Character/Narrator Development

Adult writers use a variety of techniques to develop characters, and in some cases, the persona of the narrator. They describe their physical characteristics, their personalities, their actions and gestures, their emotional reactions to events, and through dialogue and internal monologue, their internal motivations and goals. Whether narratives include real people or fictional characters, the personalities, motivations, and reactions of the narrator and the characters are often central to the development of the narrative. When children develop characters, some are "stock characters" that regularly inhabit children's stories, such as the mean teacher, the school bully, and the wicked witch. Other characters are more fully and uniquely developed through description, dialogue, and other narrative techniques.

Although children may produce narratives in which fictional characters are fairly well developed, they are less likely to develop the persona of the narrator. And, when they are producing simple recounts of events in their lives, neither the people in their narrative nor the persona of the narrator may be particularly well developed. In simple recounts, the focus is more likely to be on what people did than on their motives or reactions.

Closure

Writers bring closure to narratives in a variety of ways. Structurally, they achieve closure by providing a resolution to a problem (or a failed resolution). But they also provide closure with a variety of overt signals—with evaluations that inform the reader what the narrator thought about the events, with comments that serve to tie up loose ends in the narrative or bridge the gap between the narrative and the present, and with typical ending markers such as "the end" and "they all lived happily ever after." As children mature, their strategies for providing closure become more sophisticated and their repertoire of strategies more broad.

Narrative in First Grade

By first grade, young writers typically establish some kind of context for their narratives, albeit a very simple one. In some cases, they simply identify an occasion but not a time ("I wt to Butty and the Beste [Beauty and the Beast]."). Less advanced students may also produce writing that contains only one or two incidents loosely strung together ("I wt to Butty and the Best I bot a flowr."). Event-driven pieces, in which events follow one another without any apparent cause-and-effect relationship, are fairly common at this grade level.

Students who meet the standard establish a context. For instance, they may attempt to set the narrative in time in relation to the present ("A big time agoe when I was in keindrgareden I brohc my arem."; "It paend in October twellf twothawsind and one.").

They produce writing that reflects a plan about where in a sequence of actions the narrative should start ("One day I went to the beach and as I steped into the water tadpoles were in the water…") and stop. Their writing contains two or more appropriately sequenced events that readers can easily reconstruct. They may attempt dialogue, and they may explain the causes of events ("Days had passed and the tadpole woudent eat fishfood. With no food and no fresh air it died."). Typically, they use simple linking words to signal chronological ordering ("then"; "frst [first]"; "Then when…"; "again"; "A big time agoe…"). They frequently incorporate drawings to expand or illustrate their texts. They provide some sense of closure, often with a reflective statement ("That was the best birthday I ever had.").

Narrative Rubrics Elements

	5 **Exceeds Standard***	**4** **Meets Standard**
Orientation and Context	• Establishes a context (e.g., time, place, or occasion).	• Establishes a context (e.g., time, place, or occasion).
Plot Development and Organization	• Produces writing that reflects a plan about where in a series of incidents or events the story should start and stop. • Develops a narrative containing two or more appropriately sequenced events that readers can easily reconstruct.	• Produces writing that reflects a plan about where in a series of incidents or events the story should start and stop. • Develops a narrative containing two or more appropriately sequenced events that readers can easily reconstruct.
Character/Narrator Development	• Provides little, if any, character development.	• Provides little, if any, character development.
Closure	• Provides some sense of closure. • May include reflective statements (e.g., "I was glad to have my dog back and I will never forget to love him again.").	• Provides some sense of closure. • May include reflective statements (e.g., "I was glad to have my dog back and I will never forget to love him again.").

	3 **Needs Revision**	**2** **Needs Instruction**	**1** **Needs Substantial Support**
Orientation and Context	• Establishes a simple context (e.g., time, place, or occasion).	• Establishes a simple context (e.g., time, place, or occasion).	• Establishes a simple context (e.g., time, place, or occasion).
Plot Development and Organization	• Produces writing that reflects a plan about where in a series of incidents or events the story should start and stop. • Develops a narrative containing two or more appropriately sequenced events that readers can easily reconstruct.	• Produces writing that contains an initiating event with one incident, or two incidents or events following in sequence.	• Produces writing that contains only one incident, or two incidents or events loosely strung together.
Character/Narrator Development	• Provides little, if any, character development.	• Provides little, if any, character development.	• Provides little, if any, character development.
Closure	• Provides some sense of closure. • May include a simple reflective statement (e.g., "It was fun.").	• May provide some sense of closure. • May include a simple reflective statement (e.g., "It was fun.").	• May provide some sense of closure. • May include a simple reflective statement (e.g., "It was fun.").

*The criteria that define score points 5 and 4 are identical. This is intentional. What distinguishes a 5 from a 4 is not the presence or absence of a particular element or strategy. Rather, it is the overall quality of execution and the level of language the writer employs. Writers of score point 5 papers bring something to the text that may not be provided by instruction—a deep understanding or passion for the topic and the genre.

Narrative Rubrics Strategies

	5 Exceeds Standard*	4 Meets Standard
Detail	• Uses details to describe incidents and people.	• Uses details to describe incidents and people.
Dialogue	• May attempt dialogue.	• May attempt dialogue.
Other	• May use some simple form of literary language (e.g., "he shauted in a jinte [giant] vioes [voice]."). • Uses simple transition words, phrases, or clauses (e.g., "A big time agoe…"). • May use drawings to expand or illustrate the text.	• May use some simple form of literary language (e.g., "he shauted in a jinte [giant] vioes [voice]."). • Uses simple transition words, phrases, or clauses (e.g., "A big time agoe…"). • May use drawings to expand or illustrate the text.

	3 Needs Revision	2 Needs Instruction	1 Needs Substantial Support
Detail	• Uses details to describe incidents and people.	• Produces writing that contains few details.	• Produces writing that contains little or no detail.
Dialogue	• May attempt dialogue.	• Typically does not attempt dialogue.	• Typically does not attempt dialogue.
Other	• May use some simple form of literary language (e.g., "he shauted in a jinte [giant] vioes [voice]."). • Uses simple coordinating transitions (e.g., and, then). • May use drawings to expand or illustrate the text.	• Uses simple coordinating transitions (e.g., and, then). • May use drawings to expand or illustrate the text.	• Uses simple coordinating transitions (e.g., and, then). • May use drawings to expand or illustrate the text.

*The criteria that define score points 5 and 4 are identical. This is intentional. What distinguishes a 5 from a 4 is not the presence or absence of a particular element or strategy. Rather, it is the overall quality of execution and the level of language the writer employs. Writers of score point 5 papers bring something to the text that may not be provided by instruction—a deep understanding or passion for the topic and the genre.

Score Point 5

Narrative Student Work and Commentary: "A big time agoe when I was in Keindrgareden..."

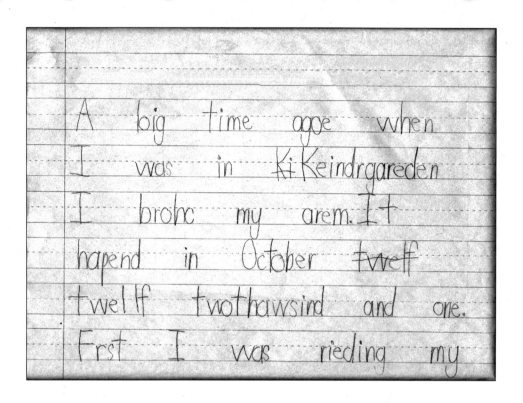

> A big time agoe when
> I was in Ki Keindrgareden
> I brohc my arem. It
> hapend in October twreff
> twellf twothawsind and one.
> Frst I was rieding my

In this piece, the writer tells the story of breaking his arm. The piece describes an extended series of events, such as riding his scooter down the sidewalk, falling down, being rescued by a neighbor, and deciding to go to the emergency room. The piece exceeds the standard for narrative at first grade.

The writer's opening sentence establishes a specific context for the piece ("A big time agoe when I was in Keindrgareden I brohc my arem. It hapend in October twellf twothawsind and one.").

The piece includes a lengthy and detailed series of events: The narrator rides his scooter up and down the sidewalk, he trips and falls, the neighbor rescues him, his mother asks if he wants to go to the hospital, he chooses the color of his cast, he gets his cast removed.

The writer keeps the reader engaged by asking and answering questions in the piece ("Can you find out how I tript? I think I tript on our nabrs short brick wall.").

The writer ends the piece by describing the machine used to remove his cast ("A masheen theat has somthing that has a thing that cots it.").

The piece includes details about the incidents he describes (the cast was on for "to week's" and the cast was "Blue").

The piece includes dialogue between the narrator and his mother ("Then my mom 'said, do you whant me to coll the immerjginse room? I 'said, yes.'").

The writer uses simple transitions ("And," "Frist").

2

Scooter down the sidewalke.
Thene I did it oll
over again. Then I got
so kereed away that I
did it so meny times.
Then when I was gowing
up the sidewalke I

Score Point 5 *continued*

3

tript. ~~eGn~~ Can you find
out how ~~iI~~ tript? I
think I tript on our
nabrs short brick wall.
And did I ~~fo~~ fall on the
street or the sidewalk?
Then our ~~nabi~~ naber pick

4

me up. Then my mom
"said, ~~do~~ you ~~what~~ whant me
to coll the inmerjginse room?
I "said, yes." I had to
hov my cast on to
weeks. It vas not fun
to hav a cast for to

Score Point 5 *continued*

5

weeks. A cast imite be fun
cus you get to pick
a caler. I pick Blue.
What will you pick?
And when I got my
cast reemoovd it ticals. Can
you f find out whawhat

6

thea yousd? A mmoosheen
theat has somthifg that
that has a thing cts cts
it.

Score Point 5 *continued*

Assessment Summary: "A big time agoe when I was in Keindrgareden…"

ELEMENTS		
	Exceeds Standard	**Commentary**
Orientation and Context	• Establishes a context (e.g., time, place, or occasion).	The writer's opening sentence establishes a specific context for the piece ("A big time agoe when I was in Keindrgareden I brohc my arem. It hapend in October twellf twothawsind and one.").
Plot Development and Organization	• Produces writing that reflects a plan about where in a series of incidents or events the story should start and stop. • Develops a narrative containing two or more appropriately sequenced events that readers can easily reconstruct.	The piece includes a lengthy and detailed series of events: The narrator rides his scooter up and down the sidewalk, he trips and falls, the neighbor rescues him, his mother asks if he wants to go to the hospital, he chooses the color of his cast, he gets his cast removed. The writer keeps the reader engaged by asking and answering questions in the piece ("Can you find out how I tript? I think I tript on our nabrs short brick wall.").
Character/ Narrator Development	• Provides little, if any, character development.	
Closure	• Provides some sense of closure. • May include reflective statements (e.g., "I was glad to have my dog back and I will never forget to love him again.").	The writer ends the piece by describing the machine used to remove his cast ("A masheen theat has somthing that has a thing that cots it.").

STRATEGIES		
	Exceeds Standard	**Commentary**
Detail	• Uses details to describe incidents and people.	The piece includes details about the incidents he describes (the cast was on for "to week's" and the cast was "Blue").
Dialogue	• May attempt dialogue.	The piece includes dialogue between the narrator and his mother ("Then my mom 'said, do you whant me to coll the immerjginse room? I 'said, yes.'").
Other	• May use some simple form of literary language (e.g., "he shauted in a jinte [giant] vioes [voice]."). • Uses simple transition words, phrases, or clauses (e.g., "A big time agoe…"). • May use drawings to expand or illustrate the text.	The writer uses simple transitions ("And," "Frist").

Note: The commentary highlights the elements and strategies in the student paper, focusing on how well the paper addresses the totality of the elements and strategies rather than on whether each is included.

Score Point 4

Narrative Student Work and Commentary: "I bot at littl coten ball"

"I bot at littl coten ball" tells the story of getting a new hamster. The piece includes a clear start and end, and the writer's discussion of her feelings develops the events she describes. "I bot at littl coten ball" represents writing that meets the first-grade standard.

The opening sentence ("I went to biye a hamster.") establishes a context for the piece.

In the piece, the girl buys the hamster, the hamster squeaks, the girl names her hamster and concludes that her hamster is soft and cuddly.

The writer includes events that the reader can reconstruct (her father teases her because the hamster squeaks; she names the hamster Niblet, explaining,

"I nameed my hamster nibllet becaus she nibls to much because she liks that.").

The piece has a concluding sentence that provides closure and echoes the title: "After I took her out she was so soft and cuddley she felt like a littll coten ball."

The writer uses detail to describe actions and incidents ("I was so excited I woted to run all the waye there..." and "she Skwet so much she suwed [sounded] like a skweing bed.").

The piece includes dialogue ("And at nite when my Dad came home he sedi wus that Noese..."), literary language (describing the hamster as a "coten ball"), and transition words ("And" and "Then").

Score Point 4 *continued*

I got a nerves hamster but I didt
know she was going to be so nerves
So we bot her that afternoon she
skwet so much she suwed like a
skweing bed. And at nite when
my Dad came home he sed i wus that
Noese I sed it is nibllet I naomeed
my hamster nibllet becaus she
nibls to much becaus she liks that
She is a difent hamster becausFlufy
was there be for that hamster but he

did becaus my bother sed that
hamster olnley live for tow yers.
but I did tek her out of the box
After I took her out she was so
soft and cuddley she felt like a littl
coten ball.

Score Point 4 *continued*

Assessment Summary: "I bot at littl coten ball"

ELEMENTS		
	Meets Standard	**Commentary**
Orientation and Context	• Establishes a context (e.g., time, place, or occasion).	The opening sentence ("I went to biye a hamster.") establishes a context for the piece.
Plot Development and Organization	• Produces writing that reflects a plan about where in a series of incidents or events the story should start and stop. • Develops a narrative containing two or more appropriately sequenced events that readers can easily reconstruct.	In the piece, the girl buys the hamster, the hamster squeaks, the girl names her hamster and concludes that her hamster is soft and cuddly. The writer includes events that the reader can reconstruct (her father teases her because the hamster squeaks; she names the hamster Niblet, explaining, "I nameed my hamster nibllet becaus she nibls to much because she liks that.").
Character/ Narrator Development	• Provides little, if any, character development.	
Closure	• Provides some sense of closure. • May include reflective statements (e.g., "I was glad to have my dog back and I will never forget to love him again.").	The piece has a concluding sentence that provides closure and echoes the title: "After I took her out she was so soft and cuddley she felt like a littll coten ball."
STRATEGIES		
	Meets Standard	**Commentary**
Detail	• Uses details to describe incidents and people.	The writer uses detail to describe actions and incidents ("I was so excited I woted to run all the waye there..." and "she Skwet so much she suwed [sounded] like a skweing bed.").
Dialogue	• May attempt dialogue.	The piece includes dialogue ("And at nite when my Dad came home he sedi wus that Noese...").
Other	• May use some simple form of literary language (e.g., "he shauted in a jinte [giant] vioes [voice]."). • Uses simple transition words, phrases, or clauses (e.g., "A big time agoe..."). • May use drawings to expand or illustrate the text.	The piece includes literary language (describing the hamster as a "coten ball"). The piece includes simple transition words ("And" and "Then").
Note: The commentary highlights the elements and strategies in the student paper, focusing on how well the paper addresses the totality of the elements and strategies rather than on whether each is included.		

Score Point 3

Narrative Student Work and Commentary: "Did you smell..."

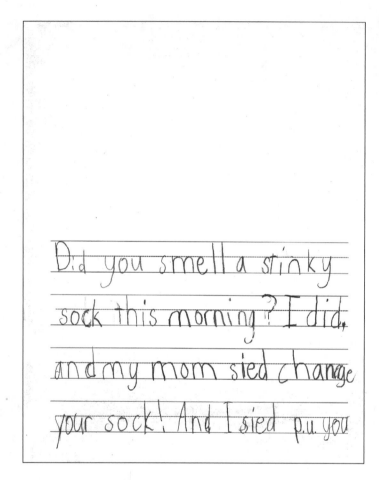

Did you smell a stinky sock this morning? I did, and my mom sied change your sock! And I sied p.u. you

In this piece, the writer tells the story of getting ready for school one morning. Because his socks are stinky, his mother wants him to change his socks and his father shouts at him. The writer tells a story that readers understand, but he loses control of the narrative near the end of the piece. The piece needs revision in order to meet the standard for first-grade narrative writing.

The writer establishes a context by beginning the story with a question ("Did you smell a stinky sock this morning? I did.").

The piece begins with the writer's question about stinky socks and ends with the boy going to school. The story includes a series of events (his Mom tells him to change his socks; his Dad shouts at him; he

leaves for school). The piece loses focus when the writer describes his encounter with his Dad because it is hard to understand what his Dad wants him to do. (The reader can infer that Dad wants the boy to hurry so they are not late for school.)

The sentence "and finite I want to school" provides a sense of closure.

The writer includes details about how stinky his sock is ("it smelled like a full socks trashcan.").

The writer attempts to use dialogue ("And I sied P.U. you stink.").

The writer uses the word "and" to provide transitions throughout the piece.

The piece includes some literary language ("he shauted in a jinte vioes").

Score Point 3 continued

stink. It smelled like a full trashcan. And it smelled like a full socks trashcan. and my dad shauted at me. And he shauted again. And seid it is time to go to school. and he shauted in a jinte vioes I carred it

with my fingusnails. And he shauted again and it tock me a hadack. ~~dy~~ shaving ~~dy~~ ~~my~~ ~~dad.~~ and finite I want to school.

Score Point 3 *continued*

Assessment Summary: "Did you smell..."

ELEMENTS		
	Needs Revision	**Commentary**
Orientation and Context	• Establishes a simple context (e.g., time, place, or occasion).	The writer establishes a context by beginning the story with a question ("Did you smell a stinky sock this morning? I did.").
Plot Development and Organization	• Produces writing that reflects a plan about where in a series of incidents or events the story should start and stop. • Develops a narrative containing two or more appropriately sequenced events that readers can easily reconstruct.	The piece begins with the writer's question about stinky socks and ends with the boy going to school. The story includes a series of events (his Mom tells him to change his socks; his Dad shouts at him; he leaves for school). The piece loses focus when the writer describes his encounter with his Dad because it is hard to understand what his Dad wants him to do. (The reader can infer that Dad wants the boy to hurry so they are not late for school.)
Character/ Narrator Development	• Provides little, if any, character development.	
Closure	• Provides some sense of closure. • May include a simple reflective statement (e.g., "It was fun.").	The sentence "and finite I want to school" provides a sense of closure.
STRATEGIES		
	Needs Revision	**Commentary**
Detail	• Uses details to describe incidents and people.	The writer includes details about how stinky his sock is ("it smelled like a full socks trashcan.").
Dialogue	• May attempt dialogue.	The writer attempts to use dialogue ("And I sied P.U. you stink.").
Other	• May use some simple form of literary language (e.g., "he shauted in a jinte [giant] vioes [voice]."). • Uses simple coordinating transitions (e.g., and, then). • May use drawings to expand or illustrate the text.	The piece includes simple literary language ("he shauted in a jinte vioes"). The writer uses the word "and" to provide transitions throughout the piece.

Note: The commentary highlights the elements and strategies in the student paper, focusing on how well the paper addresses the totality of the elements and strategies rather than on whether each is included.

Possible Conference Topics

The writer will benefit from a conference to discuss developing the events he describes, such as explaining why his father shouted at him and what he did with the stinky sock.

Score Point 2

Narrative Student Work and Commentary: "When I went camping"

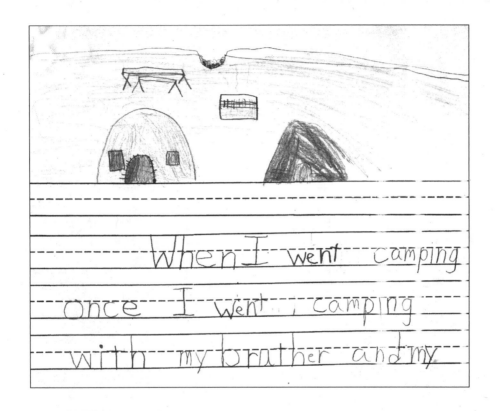

When I went camping
once I went camping
with my bruther and my

The writer of "When I went camping" needs instruction to meet the first-grade standard for narrative. The piece includes several events that happened during the writer's camping trip with his brother and father, but the story lacks details and the writer loses control over the sequence of events.

The writer establishes a context with the opening sentence of the piece ("once I went camping with my bruther and my dad.").

The piece contains an initiating event ("My dad set up the tent.") and is followed by several incidents (they catch lizards; they eat chicken for dinner; they go swimming).

The writer ends the piece with a shift in time: "the nest day we went sweming in a laKe."

The writer comments on the experience of the camping trip, saying, "I felt heappy."

The piece includes scant detail ("Zack cot a lezerd as the sis of my feeger.").

The piece does not include coordinating transitions, but does use the word "once" to begin the piece and the phrase "the nest day" to end the piece.

The piece includes a drawing of two tents and a picnic table; the drawing provides some detail about the scene that the writer does not state explicitly.

Score Point 2 continued

dad. My dad setup the
tent then Zack and
me looked for lezerds
my dad's name is
Bill. For diner was
chekm. Zack cot
a lezerd as the sis

of my feeger. I dot
utot of lezrds I
felt heappy the nes4
day we went sweming
in a laike.

$\mathscr{S}$core $\mathscr{P}$oint 2 *continued*

Assessment Summary: "When I went camping"

ELEMENTS		
	Needs Instruction	**Commentary**
Orientation and Context	• Establishes a simple context (e.g., time, place, or occasion).	The writer establishes a context with the opening sentence of the piece ("once I went camping with my bruther and my dad.").
Plot Development and Organization	• Produces writing that contains an initiating event with one incident, or two incidents or events following in sequence.	The piece contains an initiating event ("My dad set up the tent.") and is followed by several incidents (they catch lizards; they eat chicken for dinner; they go swimming).
Character/Narrator Development	• Provides little, if any, character development.	
Closure	• May provide some sense of closure. • May include a simple reflective statement (e.g., "It was fun.").	The writer ends the piece with a shift in time: "the nest day we went sweming in a laKe." The writer comments on the experience of the camping trip, saying, "I felt heappy."
STRATEGIES		
	Needs Instruction	**Commentary**
Detail	• Produces writing that contains few details.	The piece includes scant detail ("Zack cot a lezerd as the sis of my feeger.").
Dialogue	• Typically does not attempt dialogue.	
Other	• Uses simple coordinating transitions (e.g., and, then). • May use drawings to expand or illustrate the text.	The piece does not include coordinating transitions, but does use the word "once" to begin the piece and the phrase "the nest day" to end the piece. The piece includes a drawing of two tents and a picnic table; the drawing provides some detail about the scene that the writer does not state explicitly.

Note: The commentary highlights the elements and strategies in the student paper, focusing on how well the paper addresses the totality of the elements and strategies rather than on whether each is included.

Next Steps in Instruction

The writer will benefit from instruction on the following topics: planning a sequence of events to write about; adding details when describing scenes, events, people, etc.; and using transition words and phrases to create coherence and guide readers through the story.

Score Point 1

Narrative Student Work and Commentary: "I remember when me and keith..."

This piece is a very brief recount of a class's visit to a museum. The young writer does provide some details, but these do not advance the action or develop character.

The writer establishes a simple context for the piece ("when me and keith and the clas and a fue other clasis went to a musium...").

As a result of this initiating event, the writer tells us about a single incident ("I saw a piter that a lady had printid with oringei cinde [orange kind] of pante."), and there is a drawing to illustrate the text.

The piece does not include dialogue or coordinating transitions.

oringei cinde of pante I like
it

 *continued*

Assessment Summary:
"I remember when me and keith..."

ELEMENTS		
	Needs Substantial Support	**Commentary**
Orientation and Context	• Establishes a simple context (e.g., time, place, or occasion).	The writer establishes a simple context for the piece ("when me and keith and the clas and a fue other clasis went to a musium...").
Plot Development and Organization	• Produces writing that contains only one incident, or two incidents or events loosely strung together.	As a result of this initiating event, the writer tells us about a single incident ("I saw a piter that a lady had printid with oringei cinde [orange kind] of pante.").
Character/ Narrator Development	• Provides little, if any, character development.	
Closure	• May provide some sense of closure. • May include a simple reflective statement (e.g., "It was fun.").	

STRATEGIES		
	Needs Substantial Support	**Commentary**
Detail	• Produces writing that contains little or no detail.	
Dialogue	• Typically does not attempt dialogue.	
Other	• Uses simple coordinating transitions (e.g., and, then). • May use drawings to expand or illustrate the text.	There is a drawing to illustrate the text.

Note: The commentary highlights the elements and strategies in the student paper, focusing on how well the paper addresses the totality of the elements and strategies rather than on whether each is included.

Roadmap for Development

This writing is very typical at kindergarten and first grade. The writer needs support in order to write longer, more fully detailed pieces and to be able to create a series of events with a focus/central moment. This piece is clearly the work of a novice writer who will need time, practice, and instruction to mature.

Report of Information

Reports of information describe the way things are in the social and natural world. They describe classes of things, but also the components or parts of things and their relations. Reports contain various kinds of information. They answer questions such as, What are the major food groups? What is the earth made of? What role do planets play in the solar system? Reports also give information about aspects of things. They answer questions about size (How big is Texas? How tall is the Eiffel Tower?), about function (What is a telescope used for? What is a modem used for?), about behavior (What do pelicans do to find food? How do whales eat?), and about the organization of systems (What is the relationship of the House to the Senate? How is the court system organized?). Writers of this genre typically make meaning by describing and classifying things and their distinctive features. For children, this often means writing about the features of different kinds of dinosaurs, insects, planes, pets, whales, and so on. When children study science, their reports may deal with different kinds of energy, different kinds of clouds, different types of cells, etc.

Report writing poses many challenges for young students. Writing about a topic that they know well presents a different set of challenges than writing about a topic that is unfamiliar. When students know the topic, organizing the information is the primary task that consumes their energy. When they do not know the topic, gathering and phrasing the information presents additional challenges.

When students are writing about a topic they are familiar with, they can convey information in their own words and cluster information in categories that make sense to them. When they do not know the topic, they may not have the breadth or depth of understanding to analyze and categorize the information effectively. In these cases, young writers often seem to rely almost solely on headers, provided either by the teacher or by the reference materials themselves, to organize their writing.

When students do not know the topic, simply phrasing the information can be a daunting task. They must explain new information that they may not fully understand. So, the logical thing for them to do is to borrow heavily from the wording in reference books to make sure they convey correctly the ideas they are writing about. Logically, then, the syntactic patterns that emerge under these circumstances frequently are made up of some introductory, transitional, or evaluative phrasings that string together word-for-word borrowings from reference books. This is called "patch" writing and it is particularly acceptable and expected in the primary grades, where students are encouraged to mimic the language of written texts, to apprentice themselves to authors, and to borrow stylistic techniques they observe professional writers using.

The New Standards expectation for student writers in the report genre requires that they be able to craft a report that does the following: establishes a context; creates an organizing structure appropriate to audience and purpose; communicates ideas, insights, or theories that are illustrated through facts, details, quotations, statistics, and other information; uses a range of appropriate strategies to develop the text; and provides closure.

Orientation and Context

As it relates to report writing, orienting the reader usually means providing some kind of opening statement locating the subject of the paper in the universe of things. For children, the opening statement often takes the form of a definition or classification ("Whales are mammals."). Alternatively, opening statements will sometimes provide an overview of the topic ("There are many different types of whales in the ocean.") or a comment on the organization of a system ("There are three branches in the government of the United States."). Young writers also often attempt to engage reader interest in the topic by introducing startling facts or by appealing to the reader in some fashion.

Organization of Information

In reports, facts are often grouped into topic areas in a hierarchical pattern of organization such as classification. Reports also describe patterns of relations among concepts linked to facts. Although reports are often considered neutral and voiceless, in reality they convey human agendas or points of view. Thus, effective reports have a controlling idea or perspective that contributes to the organization and coherence of the text. That is, information is selected and ordered in a way that contributes to the development of the idea. Organizing information in a report also requires writers to attend to the needs of their audience, so that they provide the background information a reader would need to understand subsequent portions of the text. Writers also use paragraphing, subheads, transition words, and phrases and clauses to organize the information.

Development and Specificity of Information

There is a wide variety of ways to report information. Writers define things ("Corn is a vegetable."), give examples ("Dogs are man's best friend. Guide dogs help blind people."), and provide reasons ("My mom works on computers…I know why, she's an engineer."). Writers also explain phenomena ("Atoms are the insides of crystals…. Crystals get flat faces because the atoms form regular patterns inside."). They compare ("Some crystals are like flowers."; "Gray rabbits look like ash and smoke.") and they contrast ("Some crystals grow from lava and some grow from sea salt."). They relate cause and effect ("We used to have a dog, but my dad left the door open and he ran out into

the street."). They describe ("Dolphins have a sharp and pointed face."). They specify ("I learned a lot from doing this report. I learned about different types of dogs and breeds."). They evaluate ("All crystals are different and that's what makes them so wonderful."). The different strategies that writers use can vary from a single sentence to a chunk of text several sentences long.

In developing information in a report, effective writers provide adequate and specific information about the topic. They usually write in the present tense and exclude information that is extraneous or inappropriate. They communicate ideas, insights, and theories that are elaborated on or illustrated by facts, details, quotations, statistics, or other information. Their language is factual and precise, rather than general and non-specific. They use clear and precise descriptive language to convey distinctive features (such as shape, size, color), components (such as parts of a machine, players on a team), behaviors (such as behaviors of animals: birthing, mating, eating), uses (such as uses of soap: washing hair, washing clothes, washing cars). Frequently, writers use specialized vocabulary specifically related to the topic (such as "pride," "cubs," and "dominant male" in a paper about lion families).

Many young writers pick topics from their everyday lives that they are knowledgeable about and that lend themselves to everyday vocabulary (such as siblings, family members, the family dog). In these cases, the writing may appear less sophisticated than the writing of a student who has picked a topic that lends itself to the use of technical vocabulary. But when students work with less familiar topics, the language they use may not appear to be their own. Both situations, in their own way, make it difficult to accurately evaluate the writer's development. It is important to keep in mind, though, that young writers who are imitating the language of the books they read are in the process of making that language their own.

Closure

Although their reports may not always have a formal conclusion, as would be expected in the writing of adults, young writers typically provide some sort of closure, such as a shift from particular facts to some kind of general statement or claim about the topic ("Everything is an adventure when you have a passport. All you have to do is get one!").

Report of Information in First Grade

Like most children, first graders love to tell people about what they know. Their work often seems to say, "I have a lot of really good stuff to tell you." The range of performance for report of information in first grade is very wide. Some students may only produce a general statement or a brief list of unelaborated facts. The information they report may be limited and very general. Other students may be more fluent, but produce writing that is incoherent and lacks organization. Some young writers at this grade level may not cluster details or provide other organizing structures. For instance, the following report titled "Tiger" reveals a very early, emerging understanding of the purpose and strategies of report: "Tiger has fur Tiger Has Stripse Tiger has pos [paws] and clos [claws] Tiger rus [runs] fast." We can recognize the writer's attempt to share information about tigers, but his very brief and unelaborated list of facts is less developed than the writing of many of his peers.

Students who meet the standard at this grade gather information about a topic, sort it into major categories (killer whales, humpback whales, sperm whales, fin back whales, blue whales), and report it to others. They may use headers or chapter titles to mark sections for subtopics, or they may provide simple internal structures with beginnings, middles, and ends. These writers use concrete and specific facts to develop points ("She cooks delicios food for me to eat such as yam, rice, soup, vegtables, and apples."). They define topics and provide examples ("Farmers are people who work on the farm. They clean the animals and the farm. They give them food and water."). Report writers at first grade use everyday vocabulary, but they also use some vocabulary specifically related to the topic at hand (for instance, reports about a farm might include words like "tractor," "farmhouse," "overalls," and "hen"). Writers who meet the standard also pay attention to closure. They usually provide a conclusion, if not a simple concluding statement, sometimes by summarizing the subtopics they have addressed ("I hope you enjoyed reading about farmers.... They feed, they give the animals water they go on their tractor and plant things. That is what they do. If you want to be a farmer you have to do the same things I told you about.").

Report of Information Rubrics Elements

	5 **Exceeds Standard***	4 **Meets Standard**
Orientation and Context	• Typically announces the topic in the first sentence, or only in the title.	• Typically announces the topic in the first sentence, or only in the title.
Organization of Information	• Uses an organizational strategy such as sorting information into major categories (e.g., using headers, chapters, and pictures; or by providing a beginning, middle, and end).	• Uses an organizational strategy such as sorting information into major categories (e.g., using headers, chapters, and pictures; or by providing a beginning, middle, and end).
Development and Specificity of Information	• Reports adequate and specific facts and information pertinent to the topic. • Uses specific facts to develop points.	• Reports adequate and specific facts and information pertinent to the topic. • Uses specific facts to develop points.
Closures	• Produces some form of conclusion.	• Produces some form of conclusion.

	3 **Needs Revision**	2 **Needs Instruction**	1 **Needs Substantial Support**
Orientation and Context	• Typically announces the topic in the first sentence, or only in the title.	• Typically announces the topic in the first sentence, or only in the title.	• Typically announces the topic in the first sentence, or only in the title.
Organization of Information	• May not cluster facts or provide other organizing structure. • May use simple chapter headings that do not identify categories of information (e.g., Chapter 1). • May present information in a list.	• Typically does not cluster facts or provide other organizing structure. • May use simple chapter headings that do not identify categories of information (e.g., Chapter 1). • May present information in a list.	• Typically does not cluster facts or provide other organizing structure. • May produce a general, unelaborated statement or a simple list.
Development and Specificity of Information	• Reports facts and information about a topic. • Typically presents facts without elaboration. • May include extraneous information.	• Reports limited and general facts and information about a topic. • Typically presents facts without elaboration. • May include extraneous information.	• Makes some attempt to convey facts and information. • Provides few facts.
Closures	• Produces some form of conclusion.	• May provide a simple concluding sentence.	• May simply stop.

*The criteria that define score points 5 and 4 are identical. This is intentional. What distinguishes a 5 from a 4 is not the presence or absence of a particular element or strategy. Rather, it is the overall quality of execution and the level of language the writer employs. Writers of score point 5 papers bring something to the text that may not be provided by instruction—a deep understanding or passion for the topic and the genre.

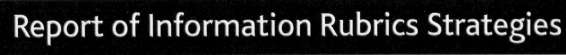

Report of Information Rubrics Strategies

	5 Exceeds Standard*		4 Meets Standard	
Names and Vocabulary	• Uses names and vocabulary related to the topic.		• Uses names and vocabulary related to the topic.	
Other	• May include illustrations or graphics to support the text.		• May include illustrations or graphics to support the text.	
	3 Needs Revision	2 Needs Instruction	1 Needs Substantial Support	
Names and Vocabulary	• Uses names and vocabulary related to the topic.	• May use names and vocabulary related to the topic.	• May use names and vocabulary related to the topic.	
Other	• May include illustrations or graphics to support the text.	• May include illustrations or graphics to support the text.	• May attempt to use illustrations or graphics to support the text.	

*The criteria that define score points 5 and 4 are identical. This is intentional. What distinguishes a 5 from a 4 is not the presence or absence of a particular element or strategy. Rather, it is the overall quality of execution and the level of language the writer employs. Writers of score point 5 papers bring something to the text that may not be provided by instruction—a deep understanding or passion for the topic and the genre.

Score Point 5

Report of Information Student Work and Commentary: "All about farmers"

"All about farmers" is a report of information that exceeds the standard for first grade. The writer uses a question-and-answer format to organize the piece, and the report includes both specific facts and elaborated ideas about farmers and farming.

The writer provides an "introduction" by explaining what led to the development of farming ("A long time ago people didn't have money to buy food and water so they had to gather food and water.").

The piece includes chapter headings in the form of questions that organize the information ("What do farmers wear"; "who are farmer"; "why do farmers work on a farm"; "Do you like farmer"). In general, the substance of each chapter answers the question posed in the heading (for instance, "Farmers are people who work on a farm. They clean the animals and the farm.").

The writer uses concrete and specific details ("They go on the tractor to plant thing like apples and banana."), and she also explains why the information is significant ("When farmer clean or feed or go on there tractors they need to wear overalls jeans and a hat so they don't get dirty.").

The piece contains a conclusion in which the writer addresses the reader directly ("I hope you enjoyed

$\mathcal{S}$core $\mathcal{P}$oint 5 *continued*

reading about farmers.... If you want to be a farmer you have to do the things I told you about.").

The piece includes vocabulary specifically related to the topic ("tractor," "overalls," "hen").

The writer includes drawings to add detail and information about farm life (including labeled pictures of animals that she does not name specifically in her text: cow, pig, horse, turkey).

Score Point 5 *continued*

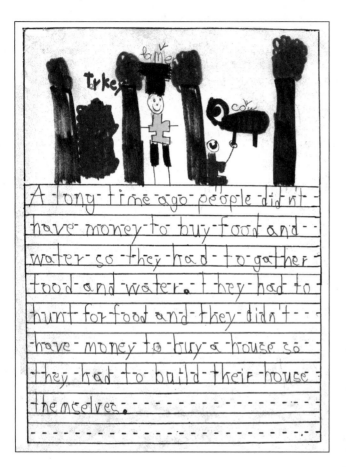

A long time ago people did'nt have money to buy food and water so they had to gather food and water. They had to hunt for food and they didn't have money to buy a house so they had to build their house themselves.

what do farmers wear when farmer clean or feed or go on there tractors they need to wear overalts jeans and a hat so they don't get dirty. When they go on there tractor or do their farm work that's how they don't get dirty

Score Point 5 *continued*

who are farmer

farmers are people who work on a
farm. they clean the animals and
the farm. They give them food and
water. They go on the tractor to
plant thing like apples and banana
They milk the cow. That is
how farmers get milk. If
farmer have cows that is

What make meat. This is
how we get meat to eat.

Score Point 5 *continued*

why do farmers work on a farm
farmers work on farms because
thats there job. They need to know
how to work on a farm and they
need to learn how to work. I know
that they feed the animals and
they clean the animals and clean
their homes.

Do you like farmer
I like farmer because I like
animals. I like the animals in
the zoo and the farm. I like
the animals in the zoo in
Africa and in other places
they live

Score Point 5 *continued*

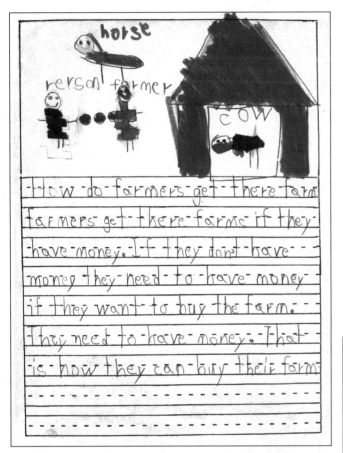

How do farmers get there farm
farmers get there farms if they
have money. If they don't have
money they need to have money
if they want to buy the farm.
They need to have money. That
is how they can buy their farm

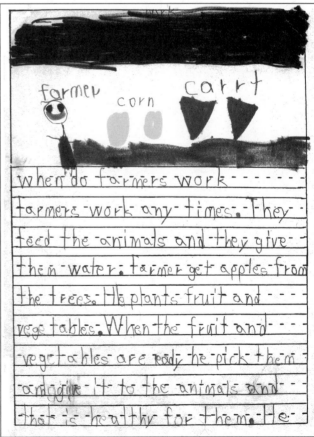

when do farmers work
farmers work any times. They
feed the animals and they give
them water. farmer get apples from
the trees. He plants fruit and
vegetables. When the fruit and
vegetables are ready he pick them
andggive it to the animals and
that is healthy for them. He

Score Point 5 *continued*

picks eggsfrom the hen
and he gos to the farmhouse
for lunch

Where do farmers live
farmers live in a farmhouse
near the form. They live with
their families. Some farmers live
in a farmhouse without their
families.

Score Point 5 *continued*

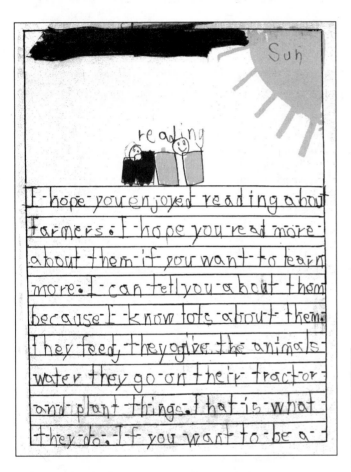

Sun

reading

I hope you enjoyed reading about farmers. I hope you read more about them if you want to learn more. I can tell you about them because I know lots about them. They feed, they give the animals water they go on their tractor and plant things. That is what they do. If you want to be a

farmer you have to do the same things I told you about.

Score Point **5** *continued*

Assessment Summary: "All about farmers"

ELEMENTS		
	Exceeds Standard	**Commentary**
Orientation and Context	• Typically announces the topic in the first sentence, or only in the title.	The writer provides an "introduction" by explaining what led to the development of farming ("A long time ago people didn't have money to buy food and water so they had to gather food and water.").
Organization of Information	• Uses an organizational strategy such as sorting information into major categories (e.g., using headers, chapters, and pictures; or by providing a beginning, middle, and end).	The piece includes chapter headings in the form of questions that organize the information ("What do farmers wear"; "who are farmer"; "why do farmers work on a farm"; "Do you like farmer"). In general, the substance of each chapter answers the question posed in the heading (for instance, "Farmers are people who work on a farm. They clean the animals and the farm.").
Development and Specificity of Information	• Reports adequate and specific facts and information pertinent to the topic. • Uses specific facts to develop points.	The writer uses concrete and specific details ("They go on the tractor to plant things like apples and banana."), and she also explains why the information is significant ("When farmer clean or feed or go on there tractors they need to wear overalls jeans and a hat so they don't get dirty.").
Closure	• Produces some form of conclusion.	The piece contains a conclusion in which the writer addresses the reader directly ("I hope you enjoyed reading about farmers … If you want to be a farmer you have to do the things I told you about.").

STRATEGIES		
	Exceeds Standard	**Commentary**
Names and Vocabulary	• Uses names and vocabulary related to the topic.	The piece includes vocabulary specifically related to the topic ("tractor," "overalls," "hen").
Other	• May include illustrations or graphics to support the text.	The writer includes drawings to add detail and information about farm life (including labeled pictures of animals that she does not name specifically in her text: cow, pig, horse, turkey).

Note: The commentary highlights the elements and strategies in the student paper, focusing on how well the paper addresses the totality of the elements and strategies rather than on whether each is included.

Score Point 4

Report of Information Student Work and Commentary: "Killer Whales"

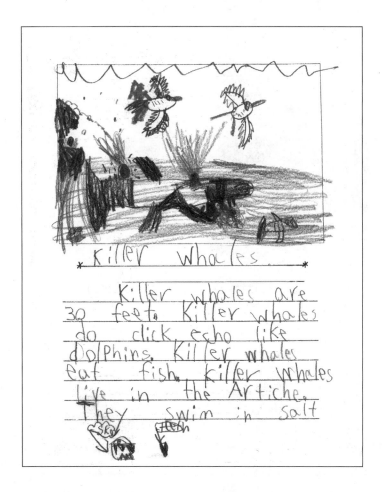

"Killer Whales" is a piece of informational writing that meets the standard for first grade. In this piece, the writer provides information about different kinds of whales, and though the report contains some repetition, it also includes a number of facts about whales.

The piece begins with a discussion of killer whales.

The piece is organized into chapters about types of whales ("Humpback Whale," "Sperm whales," "Beluga whales").

Information about each kind of whale (their size, what they eat, things they do, where they live) is presented with specific details ("30 feet," "60 feet," "real teeth," "fish and shrimp") and vocabulary specifically related to whales ("click echo," "in the Artiche," "bloe hole," "balene"). While a reader may notice some repetitions and redundancies, the report contains an impressive number of facts.

The piece concludes at the end of the writer's discussion about beluga whales ("They are cool. They have reall teeth.").

The pictures support, and in some cases, even elaborate on the text. For instance, the drawing that illustrates killer whales shows a whale spewing air and water from its blow hole, a characteristic of whales that is not mentioned in the chapter. And, although the writer does not describe the killer whale's markings in words, the distinctive black and white pattern seen in the drawing of killer whales is visible. The pictures illustrate differences among the whales.

Score Point 4 *continued*

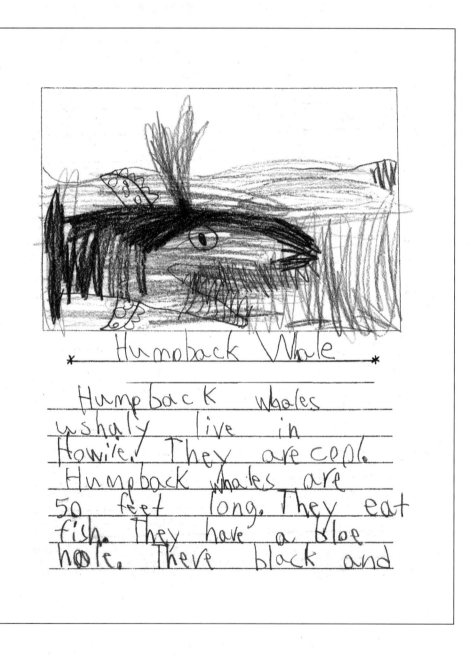

Humpback Whale

Humpback whales
ushaly live in
Howile. They are cool.
Humpback whales are
50 feet long. They eat
fish. They have a bloe
hole. There black and

Score Point 4 *continued*

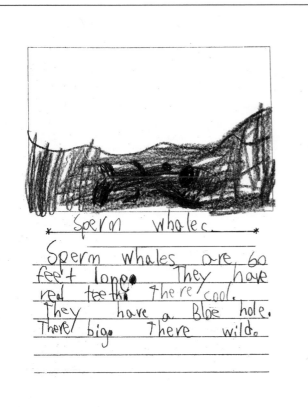

* Sperm whales. *

Sperm whales are 60
feet long. They have
real teeth. There cool.
They have a Bloe hole.
There big. There wild.

* Finback whales *

Finback whales are
80 feet long. They
are cool. They have
Balene. They eat fish
and srimp. whales are
mamals.

Score Point 4 *continued*

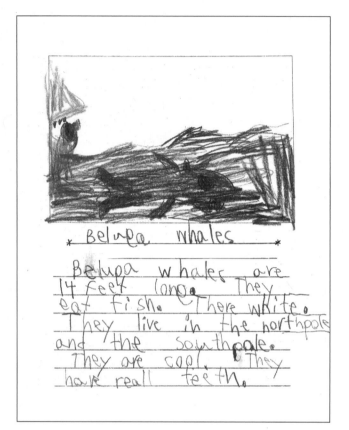

* Belupa whales *

Belupa whales are
14 feet long. They
eat fish. There white.
They live in the northpole
and the southpole.
They are cool. They
have real teeth.

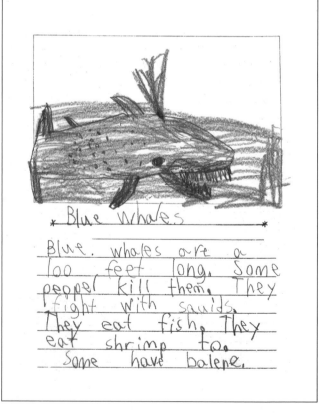

* Blue whales *

Blue whales are a
loo feet long. Some
peopel kill them. They
fight with squids.
They eat fish. They
eat shrimp to.
Some have balene.

Score Point 4 *continued*

Assessment Summary: "Killer Whales"

ELEMENTS		
	Meets Standard	**Commentary**
Orientation and Context	• Typically announces the topic in the first sentence, or only in the title.	The piece begins with a discussion of killer whales.
Organization of Information	• Uses an organizational strategy such as sorting information into major categories (e.g., using headers, chapters, and pictures; or by providing a beginning, middle, and end).	The piece is organized into chapters about types of whales ("Humpback Whale," "Sperm whales," "Beluga whales").
Development and Specificity of Information	• Reports adequate and specific facts and information pertinent to the topic. • Uses specific facts to develop points.	Information about each kind of whale (their size, what they eat, things they do, where they live) is presented with specific details ("30 feet," "60 feet," "real teeth," "fish and shrimp"). While a reader may notice some repetitions and redundancies, the report contains an impressive number of facts.
Closure	• Produces some form of conclusion.	The piece concludes at the end of the writer's discussion about beluga whales ("They are cool. They have reall teeth.").
STRATEGIES		
	Meets Standard	**Commentary**
Names and Vocabulary	• Uses names and vocabulary related to the topic.	The piece includes vocabulary specifically related to whales ("click echo," "in the Artiche," "bloe hole," "balene").
Other	• May include illustrations or graphics to support the text.	The pictures support, and in some cases, even elaborate on the text. For instance, the drawing that illustrates killer whales shows a whale spewing air and water from its blow hole, a characteristic of whales that is not mentioned in the chapter. And, although the writer does not describe the killer whale's markings in words, the distinctive black and white pattern seen in the drawing of killer whales is visible. The pictures illustrate differences among the whales.

Note: The commentary highlights the elements and strategies in the student paper, focusing on how well the paper addresses the totality of the elements and strategies rather than on whether each is included.

Score Point 3

Report of Information Student Work and Commentary: "The red fox"

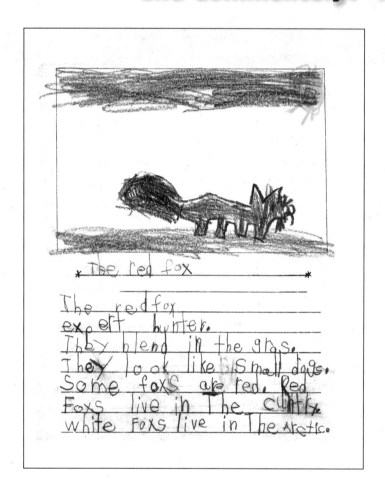

"The red fox" is an example of a paper that does not quite meet the standard. The piece reports information about foxes. The writer does not use chapter headings, but there is some internal organization to the text.

The writer announces the topic only with the title, "The red fox," and a picture of a fox.

In parts of the piece, facts and details are loosely clustered in pairs of sentences around subtopics. For instance, the first two sentences are about foxes' skills as hunters and why they are successful ("The red fox expert hunter. They blend in the gras."). The next two are about what foxes look like ("They look like small dogs. Some foxs are red."). The next sentences explain where two different kinds of foxes live ("Red foxs live in The cuntry. white Foxs live in The Arctic."). Later, a pair of sentences describe what foxes eat ("Foxs eat rabits. and They eat Fish.").

The writer elaborates on the facts he provides in his discussion of whiskers ("They have wiskers because when They dig There Wiskers tel them that Some thing is there.").

The writer concludes the piece by summing up his feelings about foxes ("I Love foxs.").

The piece includes vocabulary specifically related to the topic ("cubs," "wiskers," "Arctic").

Score Point 3 *continued*

They have wiskers
becouse wen They
dig There wiskers
+el Them that Some
thing is there.
Foxc eat rabits.
and They eat Fish.
Foxs have ba.bx cubs.
I Love Foxs.

Score Point 3 continued

Assessment Summary: "The red fox"

ELEMENTS		
	Needs Revision	**Commentary**
Orientation and Context	• Typically announces the topic in the first sentence, or only in the title.	The writer announces the topic only with the title, "The red fox," and a picture of a fox.
Organization of Information	• May not cluster facts or provide other organizing structure. • May use simple chapter headings that do not identify categories of information (e.g., Chapter 1). • May present information in a list.	In parts of the piece, facts and details are loosely clustered in pairs of sentences around subtopics.
Development and Specificity of Information	• Reports facts and information about a topic. • Typically presents facts without elaboration. • May include extraneous information.	The first two sentences are about foxes' skills as hunters and why they are successful ("The red fox expert hunter. They blend in the gras."). The next two are about what foxes look like ("They look like small dogs. Some foxs are red."). The next sentences explain where two different kinds of foxes live ("Red foxs live in The cuntry. white Foxs live in The Arctic."). Later, a pair of sentences describe what foxes eat ("Foxs eat rabits. and They eat Fish."). The writer elaborates on the facts he provides in his discussion of whiskers ("They have wiskers because when They dig There Wiskers tel them that Some thing is there.").
Closure	• Produces some form of conclusion.	The writer concludes the piece by summing up his feelings about foxes ("I Love foxs.").
STRATEGIES		
	Needs Revision	**Commentary**
Names and Vocabulary	• Uses names and vocabulary related to the topic.	The piece includes vocabulary specifically related to the topic ("cubs," "wiskers," "Arctic").
Other	• May include illustrations or graphics to support the text.	

Note: The commentary highlights the elements and strategies in the student paper, focusing on how well the paper addresses the totality of the elements and strategies rather than on whether each is included.

Possible Conference Topics

The writer will benefit from a conference to discuss some of the following topics: introducing a topic; organizing a piece with chapter headings and appropriate transitions; and adding relevant, specific, descriptive details to elaborate on the subtopics of a text.

Score Point 2

Report of Information Student Work and Commentary: "Milk"

This piece about milk is a good example of a paper at score point 2. The writer provides information about milk for readers, but the information is very general and the piece does not have an organizing structure. This writer will need instruction in order to meet the standard for a report of information at first grade.

The writer uses only the title to announce the topic for readers.

The piece provides limited and general information about milk ("MiLk Comes from Cows."; "you cot Make Milk into ice cream.").

The writer does not cluster details or provide other organizing structures such as chapter headings, and she has difficulty maintaining a focus. Her focus shifts abruptly from things you can make from milk (ice cream, chocolate milk, yogurt) and milk's effect on growth, to extraneous information about when "they" milk the cows ("every Saturday ANd Sundays") and what cows say ("moo"). In the next sentence, the piece returns briefly to the subject of milk ("White is the Color of milk." and "you cot Pot miLK to your cerieL."), but then shifts focus again with the sentence about the color of snow, which is "White Just like MiLK."

The writer concludes with a comment about the value of drinking milk ("If you don't have Milk You can't grow Strong BoNS.").

The writer uses vocabulary related to the topic ("yogurt," "ceriel").

The fact that the writer calls this piece a "story" and has difficulty maintaining a focus suggests that she is just beginning to understand the elements and strategies of report.

Score Point 2 continued

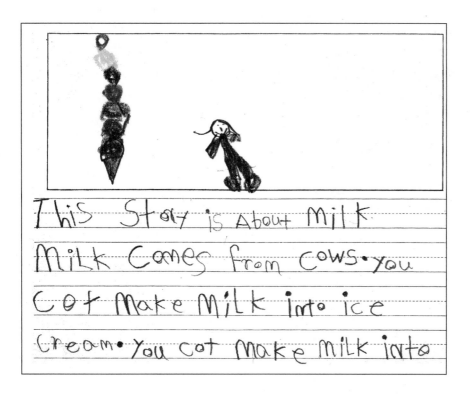

This Story is About Milk
Milk Comes from cows.you
Cot make Milk into ice
cream.you cot make milk into

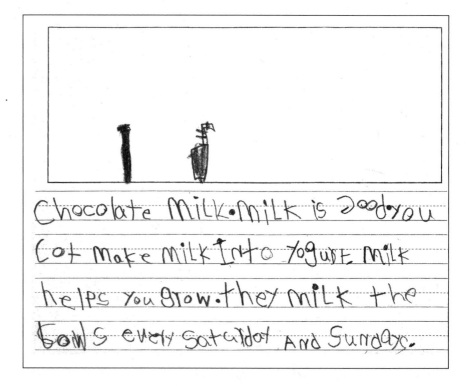

Chocolate milk.milk is Jood.you
Cot make milk Into Yogure.milk
helps you grow.they milk the
Cows every Sataday And Sundays.

Score Point 2 *continued*

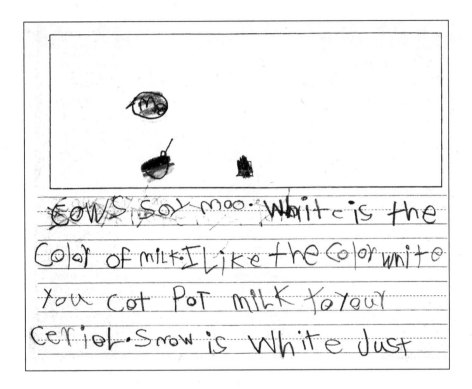

Cows say moo. White is the color of milk. I Like the color white you cot Pot milk to your cerioL. Snow is white just

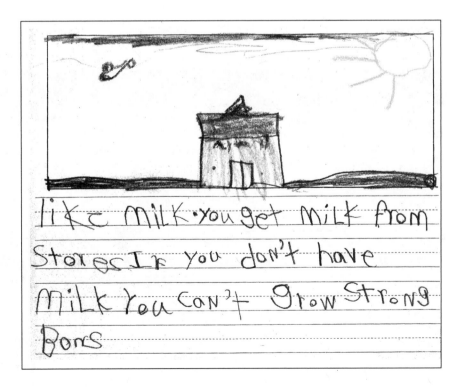

like milk. you get milk from stores. If you don't have milk you can't grow strong Bons.

Score Point **2** *continued*

Assessment Summary: "Milk"

ELEMENTS		
	Needs Instruction	**Commentary**
Orientation and Context	• Typically announces the topic in the first sentence, or only in the title.	The writer uses only the title to announce the topic for readers. The fact that the writer calls this piece a "story" and has difficulty maintaining a focus suggests that she is just beginning to understand the elements and strategies of report.
Organization of Information	• Typically does not cluster facts or provide other organizing structure. • May use simple chapter headings that do not identify categories of information (e.g., Chapter 1). • May present information in a list.	The writer does not cluster details or provide other organizing structures such as chapter headings, and she has difficulty maintaining a focus. Her focus shifts abruptly from things you can make from milk (ice cream, chocolate milk, yogurt) and milk's effect on growth, to extraneous information about when "they" milk the cows ("every Saturday ANd Sundays") and what cows say ("moo"). In the next sentence, the piece returns briefly to the subject of milk ("White is the Color of milk." and "you cot Pot miLK to your cerieL."), but then shifts focus again with the sentence about the color of snow, which is "White Just like MiLK."
Development and Specificity of Information	• Reports limited and general facts and information about a topic. • Typically presents facts without elaboration. • May include extraneous information.	The piece provides limited and general information about milk ("MiLk Comes from Cows."; "you cot Make Milk into ice cream.").
Closure	• May provide a simple concluding sentence.	The writer concludes with a comment about the value of drinking milk ("If you don't have Milk You can't grow Strong BoNS.").
STRATEGIES		
	Needs Instruction	**Commentary**
Names and Vocabulary	• May use names and vocabulary related to the topic.	The writer uses vocabulary related to the topic ("yogurt," "ceriel").
Other	• May include illustrations or graphics to support the text.	
Note: The commentary highlights the elements and strategies in the student paper, focusing on how well the paper addresses the totality of the elements and strategies rather than on whether each is included.		

Next Steps in Instruction

The writer will benefit from instruction on the following topics: distinguishing between narrative and report writing, introducing a topic, clustering information in subtopics, and elaborating on information.

Score Point 1

Report of Information Student Work and Commentary: "on esr..."

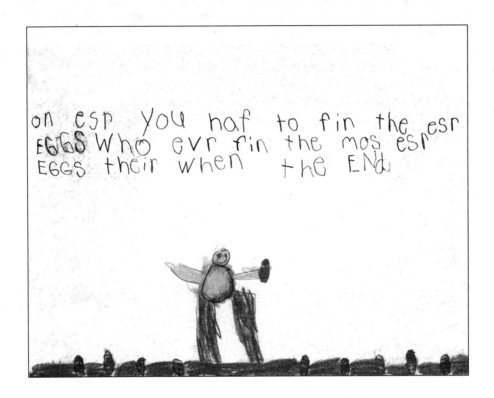

This piece represents the very early beginnings of a writer's understanding of a report of information. The piece contains only two pieces of information and an accompanying illustration.

The writer communicates the topic to readers in the first sentence.

The writer attempts to convey information to readers ("on esr [Easter] you haf to fin the esr [Easter] EGGS Who evr fin the mas esr [Easter] EGGS their [they] when [win]"). The information provided is very general and unelaborated.

The writer provides closure with the phrase "the ENd."

The piece includes a picture of a child with Easter eggs; the picture supports the text.

Score Point 1 *continued*

Assessment Summary: "on esr..."

ELEMENTS		
	Needs Substantial Support	**Commentary**
Orientation and Context	• Typically announces the topic in the first sentence, or only in the title.	The writer communicates the topic to readers in the first sentence.
Organization of Information	• Typically does not cluster facts or provide other organizing structure. • May produce a general, unelaborated statement or a simple list.	See commentary below.
Development and Specificity of Information	• Makes some attempt to convey facts and information. • Provides few facts.	The writer attempts to convey information to readers ("on esr [Easter] you haf to fin the esr [Easter] EGGS Who evr fin the mas esr [Easter] EGGS their [they] when [win]"). The information provided is very general and unelaborated.
Closure	• May simply stop.	The writer provides closure with the phrase "the ENd."
STRATEGIES		
	Needs Substantial Support	**Commentary**
Names and Vocabulary	• May use names and vocabulary related to the topic.	
Other	• May attempt to use illustrations or graphics to support the text.	The piece includes a picture of a child with Easter eggs; the picture supports the text.
Note: The commentary highlights the elements and strategies in the student paper, focusing on how well the paper addresses the totality of the elements and strategies rather than on whether each is included.		

Roadmap for Development

The writer needs time to develop fluency. The writer also needs access to simple informational texts to help her become more familiar with the genre, as well as ongoing support from classmates to help her provide more detail in her writing.

Instructions (sometimes called procedures, functional writing, or process essays) tell readers how to do something or describe how something is done through a sequence of actions. Beverly Derewianka (1990) explains that this genre is very important in our society because it makes it possible for us to get things done. There are many subgenres of this kind of writing: appliance manuals, science experiments, craft instructions, recipes, directions to reach a destination or to build a model, game rules, etc. In school, this type of writing appears frequently in science, homemaking, art, and other classes that focus on processes as opposed to things.

Instructions are like narratives because they are basically chronological in structure; however, instructions describe steps in a process instead of events in time. Because they are chronological in structure, children who write narratives can easily learn how to organize this genre. Young writers usually have little, if any, difficulty sequencing the steps in a plan of action.

Instructions require students to have expertise they can draw on. Fortunately, students have much expertise, even at the primary level. They know how to play games, care for pets, carve pumpkins, make peanut butter sandwiches, and so on. Having something to write about is not a problem for children who write this genre. However, the degree of specificity required sometimes makes writing instructions difficult, as does the problem of engaging the reader. Very young writers will sometimes adopt a narrative stance, presenting steps as actions they take or have taken ("I plant a sed [seed]. I water my sed [seed]. I wat far a rot [waited for a root]."). But when students see good examples of instructions, and model their own text on the examples, they are less likely to simply recount. Some topics are simply much more difficult for young writers than others. Topics that are too broad or detailed (for instance, how to play soccer, how to build a model car) are often too difficult for students, especially for those whose writing generally does not meet the standard.

Orientation and Context

There is no single way to begin instructions, but at the very least, writers must identify the activity or process and the goal. Writers of this genre also provide context, both in the beginning and throughout the text. They may explain why actions are necessary or why steps have to be taken in a particular order. They may include comments on the significance, usefulness, entertainment value, or danger of the activity in order to engage the reader. Typically, young writers of this genre also establish their credentials. That is, they create a knowledgeable stance. In texts by adult writers of this genre, a knowledgeable stance is often assumed. In the case of young writers, pictures may play a large role in providing both context and essential information.

Organization and Development of Instructions

Like narratives, instructions are organized by time. But instead of events, steps in a process or activity are the deep structure for organization. The text is organized by a sequence of actions. Typically, writers begin with the first step in the process and proceed in time until the last step. Goals are identified, materials are listed, typically in order of use, and steps oriented toward achieving the goal are described.

Writers elaborate on and organize steps in the process in a variety of ways (for example, by providing diagrams, giving reasons for actions, and creating visual imagery through words and illustrations). They create expectations through the use of predictable structures. Headings, subheadings, numbers, etc. are often used to make the process easy to understand and follow. Because instructions are organized by steps in time, common linking words are used (before, during, after, first of all, finally, next, later, simultaneously, subsequently, immediately following, in the meantime). Writers also use transition phrases to make their instructions clear and easy to follow ("When you're all done with that…"). The reader is typically referred to in a general way (one/you), but sometimes the reader is not mentioned at all if the writer uses commands to signal the steps to take ("Take the top off the hamster cage.").

When writing in this genre, successful writers provide a specific guide to action (or a specific description of the activity). They describe the steps or key components in detail, anticipating a reader's need for information and foreseeing likely points of confusion. They explain what to do, and how and why to do it ("Always try to give your hamster food at the same time each day. Then they can learn how to get up at the same time each day."). Sometimes they comment on who would need to know how to do the activity. They explain precautions that should be taken and warn about possible difficulties. They anticipate places where problems are likely to occur ("Food bowl heavy enough so the hamster can't pick it up"; "Don't give them citrus fruits, Onions, or garlic.").

Effective writers of this genre provide specific details (to explain how, what, where, and when), and they adjust the level of detail to fit the goal. They use diagrams or illustrations as complements and to supplement the verbal information in the text. They describe materials, tools, and preparations needed to carry out the process, providing precise information about size, length, weight, number, types, and so on. They define technical terms and explain steps in the process.

Closure

Often the last step of the process is the conclusion of the writing. Although instructions may not always have a formal conclusion, writers typically provide some sort of closure. Sometimes writers explain the significance of the process or summarize the main steps. Young writers sometimes use a simple concluding statement to say how one could use the results if the process leads to a product ("Maybe if you make enough you can sell them to people…"). Sometimes they simply exhort the reader to engage in the activity ("Now that you know something about Wakeboarding, get out their and wakeboard!").

Instructions in First Grade

Children in first grade delight in telling others how to do things. But within a particular class, the range of performance in writing instructions will be wide. Children who have little experience with this genre may introduce the topic only with the title, and they may not provide closure to their writing. They often present steps as a series of simple commands, without signaling the order of the steps with transition words (for example, first, next, then). They may number these simple commands, as did one young boy who wrote about how to tie your shoes ("Step 1 hoses [hold] the string together Step 2 Put the sting throgh the hole Step 3 Make a rabbit ear Step 4 Make another rabbit ear Step 5 Put the rabbit ear trough the other Step 6. And now we have a well tied shoe"). They may provide steps that are out of sequence, omit important steps, or write instructions that are too general to follow. For instance, a writer might say, "Then you start to carve the pumpkin," but give no instructions on how to carve it. They may cast steps in the past tense, recounting the experience as if it is something they have done. They typically provide few details, which they illustrate in their drawings, and they may not provide closure.

Writers who meet the standard at first grade are able to give instructions and describe, in appropriate sequence and with a few details, the steps one must take to make or do a particular thing. They may provide some kind of context for the procedure ("I am going to tell you how to draw a turkey. I chose to draw a turkey because they are funny then they go gobble."). They may number the steps or use simple transition words to signal the sequence. They usually provide details about the materials needed ("First you need a pencil and a piece of paper.") and include information to help the reader follow the steps ("Next draw a little circle for a head, on top of the stomach."). They give the steps in sequence, and while they may sometimes use commands, their sentences may also have complex structures that help them explain how to accomplish the steps ("With your pencil draw a big circle. After trace your hand to make the feathres, on top of the stomach."). If they supply drawings or other graphics, these illustrate the text. Typically, they provide closure ("Finally you can color, have fun drawing a turkey.").

Instructions Rubrics Elements

	5 Exceeds Standard*	4 Meets Standard
Orientation and Context	• May introduce the topic. • May provide context for the instructions.	• May introduce the topic. • May provide context for the instructions.
Organization and Development of Instructions	• Provides a series of general steps or actions in chronological sequence. • Provides enough information to give the reader a general sense of what is involved in the task or activity. • Provides details that help the reader understand the instructions.	• Provides a series of general steps or actions in chronological sequence. • Provides enough information to give the reader a general sense of what is involved in the task or activity. • Provides details that help the reader understand the instructions.
Closure	• Provides a sense of completeness, if not closure.	• Provides a sense of completeness, if not closure.

	3 Needs Revision	2 Needs Instruction	1 Needs Substantial Support
Orientation and Context	• May introduce the topic only with the title.	• May introduce the topic only with the title.	• May introduce the topic only with the title.
Organization and Development of Instructions	• Provides a series of very general steps or actions in chronological sequence. • Provides enough information to give the reader a general sense of what is involved in the task. • Provides some details to help readers understand the instructions.	• Provides a series of very general steps or actions. • May provide steps or actions that are out of sequence or too general to follow. • May omit important steps. • Provides few details to help readers understand the instructions.	• Provides very general steps or actions. • May provide steps or actions that are out of sequence or too general to follow. • May omit important steps. • Provides few, if any, details to help readers understand the instructions. • May cast steps in the past tense.
Closure	• May provide closure or a sense of completeness.	• May provide closure or a sense of completeness.	• May provide closure or a sense of completeness.

*The criteria that define score points 5 and 4 are identical. This is intentional. What distinguishes a 5 from a 4 is not the presence or absence of a particular element or strategy. Rather, it is the overall quality of execution and the level of language the writer employs. Writers of score point 5 papers bring something to the text that may not be provided by instruction—a deep understanding or passion for the topic and the genre.

Instructions Rubrics Strategies

	5 Exceeds Standard*	4 Meets Standard	
Transition Devices	• Uses simple transition words to indicate sequence of steps (e.g., first, next, then) • May number the steps.	• Uses simple transition words to indicate sequence of steps (e.g., first, next, then). • May number the steps.	
Other	• May use drawing or graphics to illustrate the instructions.	• May use drawings or graphics to illustrate the instructions.	

	3 Needs Revision	2 Needs Instruction	1 Needs Substantial Support
Transition Devices	• May use simple transition words (e.g., first, then). • May number the steps.	• May use simple transition words (e.g., first, then). • May number the steps.	• Typically presents steps as a series of simple commands without transition words. • May number the steps.
Other	• May rely on drawings to provide detail.	• May rely on drawings to provide detail.	• If drawings or graphics are present, they may not illustrate the instructions.

*The criteria that define score points 5 and 4 are identical. This is intentional. What distinguishes a 5 from a 4 is not the presence or absence of a particular element or strategy. Rather, it is the overall quality of execution and the level of language the writer employs. Writers of score point 5 papers bring something to the text that may not be provided by instruction—a deep understanding or passion for the topic and the genre.

Score Point 5

Instructions Student Work and Commentary: "How to Draw a Turkey"

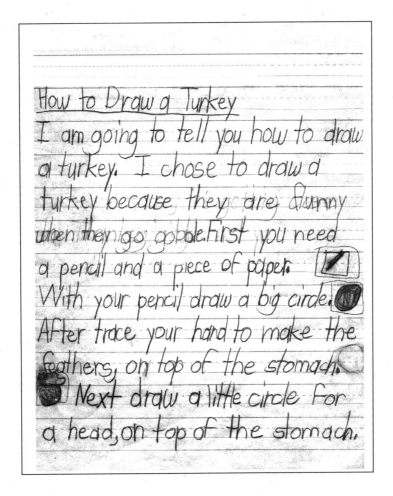

How to Draw a Turkey
I am going to tell you how to draw
a turkey. I chose to draw a
turkey because they are funny
when they go gobble. First you need
a pencil and a piece of paper.
With your pencil draw a big circle.
After trace your hand to make the
feathers, on top of the stomach.
Next draw a little circle for
a head, on top of the stomach.

The carefully illustrated piece "How to Draw a Turkey" exceeds the standard for writing instructions in first grade. The writer provides clear directions for drawing a turkey that the reader could follow.

The writer introduces the topic and provides a context for the procedure ("I am going to tell you how to draw a turkey. I chose to draw a turkey because they are funny when they go gobble.").

The piece then includes a series of steps in sequence. First, the writer includes a list of materials that the reader will need to complete the task ("First you need a pencil and a piece of paper."). She continues by describing a series of steps that are organized by time. The instructions include specific details to help the reader through the process ("Next draw a little circle for a head, on top of the stomach.").

The piece includes a closing sentence ("Finally you can color, have fun drawing a turkey.").

The piece includes transition words to help give the piece coherence ("First," "After," and "Next").

Each step includes a drawing that illustrates the directions for readers, and the combination of written instructions and illustrations provides the reader with enough detail to follow the instructions.

Score Point 5 continued

After that draw two tiny dots for eyes, in the middle of the head. Then draw a pointy beak in the middle of the head. Now it's time to draw the curved gobble, Right on the side of the beak. After draw some feet on the bottom of the stomach. Also draw wings by the sides of the stomach. finally you can color, have fun drawing a turkey.

Score Point 5 continued

Assessment Summary: "How to Draw a Turkey"

ELEMENTS		
	Exceeds Standard	**Commentary**
Orientation and Context	• May introduce the topic. • May provide context for the instructions.	The writer introduces the topic and provides a context for the procedure ("I am going to tell you how to draw a turkey. I chose to draw a turkey because they are funny when they go gobble.").
Organization and Development of Instructions	• Provides a series of general steps or actions in chronological sequence. • Provides enough information to give the reader a general sense of what is involved in the task or activity. • Provides details that help the reader understand the instructions.	The piece then includes a series of steps in sequence. First, the writer includes a list of materials that the reader will need to complete the task ("First you need a pencil and a piece of paper."). She continues by describing a series of steps that are organized by time. The instructions include specific details to help the reader through the process ("Next draw a little circle for a head, on top of the stomach.").
Closure	• Provides a sense of completeness, if not closure.	The piece includes a closing sentence ("Finally you can color, have fun drawing a turkey.").
STRATEGIES		
	Exceeds Standard	**Commentary**
Transition Devices	• Uses simple transition words to indicate sequence of steps (e.g., first, next, then). • May number the steps.	The piece includes transition words to help give the piece coherence ("First," "After," and "Next").
Other	• May use drawings or graphics to illustrate the instructions.	Each step includes a drawing that illustrates the directions for readers, and the combination of written instructions and illustrations provides the reader with enough detail to follow the instructions.

Note: The commentary highlights the elements and strategies in the student paper, focusing on how well the paper addresses the totality of the elements and strategies rather than on whether each is included.

Score Point 4

Instructions Student Work and Commentary: "How to Wrap a Present"

"How to Wrap a Present" is an example of a paper that meets the standard for writing instructions in first grade. The writer uses words and pictures to explain to readers how to wrap and give a gift.

The writer uses the title to announce the topic.

The piece includes a series of steps that give the reader a general sense of what is involved in wrapping a gift. The steps are presented in an appropriate order. Sentences such as "Get a bag" and "Then put a ribbon on the frunt" communicate a general idea about the task involved but do not include descriptive details, such as the type or color of the bag or ribbon.

The final sentence ("Then she will put it in her room.") provides a sense of completeness.

The piece includes transition words ("Then" and "Next").

The piece includes pictures that illustrate each step and help communicate the instructions to readers.

Score Point 4 continued

Get a bag. ___ put
a ___
___ the ___

Then put a toy in
the bag.

Next put a tie on the frunt.

Then put a ribbon on the frunt.

Score Point 4 *continued*

Then give it to the
prsen.

Then the prsen will
open it.

Score Point 4 *continued*

Then she will put it
in her room.

Then the prsen can
play with it.

Score Point **4** continued

Assessment Summary:
"How to Wrap a Present"

ELEMENTS		
	Meets Standard	**Commentary**
Orientation and Context	• May introduce the topic. • May provide context for the instructions.	The writer uses the title to announce the topic.
Organization and Development of Instructions	• Provides a series of general steps or actions in chronological sequence. • Provides enough information to give the reader a general sense of what is involved in the task or activity. • Provides details that help the reader understand the instructions.	The piece includes a series of steps that give the reader a general sense of what is involved in wrapping a gift. The steps are presented in an appropriate order. Sentences such as "Get a bag" and "Then put a ribbon on the frunt" communicate a general idea about the task involved but do not include descriptive details, such as the type or color of the bag or ribbon.
Closure	• Provides a sense of completeness, if not closure.	The final sentence ("Then she will put it in her room.") provides a sense of completeness.

STRATEGIES		
	Meets Standard	**Commentary**
Transition Devices	• Uses simple transition words to indicate sequence of steps (e.g., first, next, then). • May number the steps.	The piece includes transition words ("Then" and "Next").
Other	• May use drawings or graphics to illustrate the instructions.	The piece includes pictures that illustrate each step and help communicate the instructions to readers.

Note: The commentary highlights the elements and strategies in the student paper, focusing on how well the paper addresses the totality of the elements and strategies rather than on whether each is included.

Score Point 3

Instructions Student Work and Commentary: "How to Jrow a Shork"

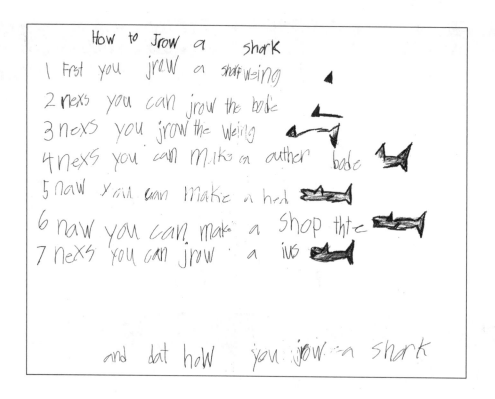

In "How to Jrow a Shork," the writer uses a combination of written text and drawings to teach readers how to draw a picture of a shark. This piece of writing shows significant promise, but it needs revision in order to meet the standard.

The author announces the topic only with the title.

The piece provides a series of general steps for drawing a shark (fin, back, tail, body, etc.).

The written instructions are so general that the reader might have to infer the meaning ("frst you jrow a shorp weing."), but the drawings that illustrate the steps provide some of the details that are not included in the written instructions. For instance, the writer does not use adjectives such as "curved" or "pointy" to describe the body or fins, but the drawings illustrate those details for readers.

The sentence "and dat how you jrow a shark" gives the piece a sense of completeness.

The writer creates coherence by numbering the steps and by including transition words ("Frst" and "Nexs").

Assessment Summary: "How to Jrow a Shork"

ELEMENTS		
	Needs Revision	**Commentary**
Orientation and Context	• May introduce the topic only with the title.	The author announces the topic only with the title.
Organization and Development of Instructions	• Provides a series of very general steps or actions in chronological sequence. • Provides enough information to give the reader a general sense of what is involved in the task. • Provides some details to help readers understand the instructions.	The piece provides a series of general steps for drawing a shark (fin, back, tail, body, etc.). The written instructions are so general that the reader might have to infer the meaning ("frst you jrow a shorp weing."), but the drawings that illustrate the steps provide some of the details that are not included in the written instructions. For instance, the writer does not use adjectives such as "curved" or "pointy" to describe the body or fins, but the drawings illustrate those details for readers.
Closure	• May provide closure or a sense of completeness.	The sentence "and dat how you jrow a shark" gives the piece a sense of completeness.
STRATEGIES		
	Needs Revision	**Commentary**
Transition Devices	• May use simple transition words (e.g., first, then). • May number the steps.	The writer creates coherence by numbering the steps and by including transition words ("Frst" and "Nexs").
Other	• May rely on drawings to provide detail.	

Note: The commentary highlights the elements and strategies in the student paper, focusing on how well the paper addresses the totality of the elements and strategies rather than on whether each is included.

Possible Conference Topics

The writer will benefit from a conference to discuss some of the following topics: providing a context for the instructions, ordering the instructions, and elaborating on the instructions by adding descriptive details.

Score Point 2

Instructions Student Work and Commentary: "Jack-o-Lanter"

Jack-o-Lanter
First you go to
the pumpkin pach
and pick a pumpkin
Then you get some
news paper and
put it on the floor

"How to Carve a Pumpkin" is a popular topic for writing assignments in the fall. "Jack-o-Lanter" tells readers how to carve a pumpkin, and the piece includes some, but not all, of the steps involved in carving a pumpkin. The author of "Jack-o-Lanter" will need instruction in order to meet the standard for writing instructions in first grade.

The writer introduces the topic with the title and a drawing of three carved pumpkins.

The piece provides a series of general steps involved in carving a pumpkin ("Then you get some newspaper and put it on the floor."). The steps are in sequence, but the writer omits significant steps (such as cutting a hole in the top of the pumpkin). Also, some of the

Score Point 2 *continued*

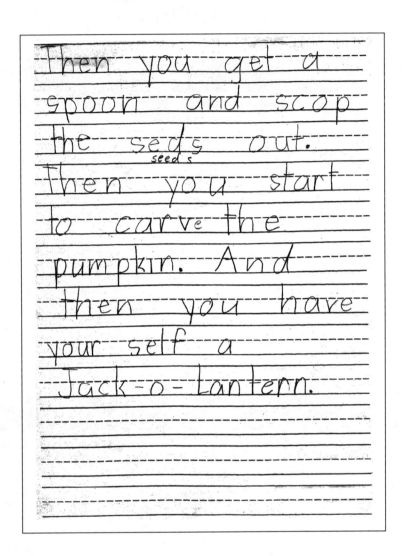

Then you get a
spoon and scop
the seds out.
seeds
Then you start
to carve the
pumpkin. And
then you have
your self a
Jack-o-Lantern.

instructions may be too general to follow. For instance, the writer says, "Then you start to carv the pumpkin," but does not offer instructions about how to carve it.

The piece does not include descriptive details (such as "big" or "orange").

The final sentence provides a sense of closure ("And then you have your self a Jack-o-Lantern.").

The writer makes the text coherent through the use of simple transition words ("First," "Then," "And"), and the transition words help guide the reader through the process.

The pictures of three jack o' lanterns at the top of the page help illustrate the instructions.

Assessment Summary: "Jack-o-Lanter"

ELEMENTS		
	Needs Instruction	**Commentary**
Orientation and Context	• May introduce the topic only with the title.	The writer introduces the topic with the title and a drawing of three carved pumpkins.
Organization and Development of Instructions	• Provides a series of very general steps or actions. • May provide steps or actions that are out of sequence or too general to follow. • May omit important steps. • Provides few details to help readers understand the instructions.	The piece provides a series of general steps involved in carving a pumpkin ("Then you get some newspaper and put it on the floor."). The steps are in sequence, but the writer omits significant steps (such as cutting a hole in the top of the pumpkin). Also, some of the instructions may be too general to follow. For instance, the writer says, "Then you start to carv the pumpkin," but does not offer instructions about how to carve it. The piece does not include descriptive details (such as "big" or "orange").
Closure	• May provide closure or a sense of completeness.	The final sentence provides a sense of closure ("And then you have your self a Jack-o-Lantern.").
STRATEGIES		
	Needs Instruction	**Commentary**
Transition Devices	• May use simple transition words (e.g., first, then). • May number the steps.	The writer makes the text coherent through the use of simple transition words ("First," "Then," "And"), and the transition words help guide the reader through the process.
Other	• May rely on drawings to provide detail.	The pictures of three jack o' lanterns at the top of the page help illustrate the instructions.

Note: The commentary highlights the elements and strategies in the student paper, focusing on how well the paper addresses the totality of the elements and strategies rather than on whether each is included.

Next Steps in Instruction

The writer will benefit from instruction on brainstorming about the different steps involved in a task and revising a piece to add descriptive words and phrases.

Score Point 1

Instructions Student Work and Commentary: "How to tie your shoes"

How to
yours hoe tie

The writer of "How to tie your shoes" demonstrates an awareness of the elements of writing instructions, but she will need support in order to meet the standard at first grade.

The writer uses only the title to introduce the topic.

The instructions include six numbered steps for tying a shoe. The writer presents the steps as simple commands ("Put the sting throgh the hole."). The steps she describes are too general to follow, and the writer omits important information. For instance, she tells readers to "Make a rabbit ear," but she does not explain what she means by the term, and she does not provide a drawing to illustrate a rabbit ear for readers.

The final step provides closure ("Step 6 And now we have a well tied shoe.").

Each step is numbered ("Step 1," "Step 2").

The piece includes a pictures of an "Automatic Shoe tier" and a tied shoe.

Score Point 1 *continued*

How to tie your shoes

Automatic
Shoe
tier

Step 1 Cross the string together
Step 2 Put the sting through
the hole Step 3 Make a rabbit ear
Step 4 Make another rabbit ear

Step 5 Put the rabbit ear trough the
other Step 6 And now we have a well
tied shoe.

Score Point **1** *continued*

Assessment Summary: "How to tie your shoes"

ELEMENTS		
	Needs Substantial Support	**Commentary**
Orientation and Context	• May introduce the topic only with the title.	The writer uses only the title to introduce the topic.
Organization and Development of Instructions	• Provides very general steps or actions. • May provide steps or actions that are out of sequence or too general to follow. • May omit important steps. • Provides few, if any, details to help readers understand the instructions. • May cast steps in the past tense.	The instructions include six numbered steps for tying a shoe. The steps she describes are too general to follow, and the writer omits important information. For instance, she tells readers to "Make a rabbit ear," but she does not explain what she means by the term, and she does not provide a drawing to illustrate a rabbit ear for readers.
Closure	• May provide closure or a sense of completeness.	The final step provides closure ("Step 6 And now we have a well tied shoe.").
STRATEGIES		
	Needs Substantial Support	**Commentary**
Transition Devices	• Typically presents steps as a series of simple commands without transition words. • May number the steps.	The writer presents the steps as simple commands ("Put the sting throgh the hole."). Each step is numbered ("Step 1," "Step 2").
Other	• If drawings or graphics are present, they may not illustrate the instructions.	The piece includes pictures of an "Automatic Shoe tier" and a tied shoe.

Note: The commentary highlights the elements and strategies in the student paper, focusing on how well the paper addresses the totality of the elements and strategies rather than on whether each is included.

Roadmap for Development

The writer will benefit from work to develop fluency. The piece is short and includes few details, and the writer will benefit from practice with developing ideas and communicating them in writing. In addition, the student will benefit from instruction on adding enough details to help readers understand the instructions.

Response to Literature

The responding to literature genre assessed by New Standards is recognized and assessed in many districts and states throughout the United States, and like other genres, it provides a rough template that defines expectations for a particular kind of writing. But it is important to note that it is only one of several ways that readers and writers respond to literature and only one of several encouraged by teachers in school. Responding to literature can take many different forms. All of them are valuable in a language arts curriculum.

Students may respond in writing to literature in a variety of ways and for a variety of purposes: to express their emotional reactions, clarify their thinking or attitudes, explore difficulties in their understanding, or simply to share their opinions with others to build a social relationship. Teachers sometimes design classroom activities that invite informal, imaginative responses wherein the focus is on helping children make connections to their own experiences and to other texts or authors they have read. Such connections deepen children's understanding.

In the classroom, the development of more formal responses is supported both by these kinds of activities and by Accountable Talk[SM]. Accountable Talk offers a set of tools for helping teachers lead academically productive group discussions. Accountable Talk is not empty chatter; it seriously responds to and further develops what others say, whether the talk occurs one-on-one, in small groups, or with the whole class. When they engage in Accountable Talk, students learn to introduce and ask for knowledge that is accurate and relevant to the text under discussion. They learn to use evidence from the text in ways that are appropriate and follow established norms of good reasoning.

Built on this kind of scaffolding, formal written responses require students to examine texts thoughtfully and to draw evidence from them to make assertions and substantiate arguments. A good response to literature is never built on unsupported opinion. Polished and crafted for an audience, effective papers in this genre always demonstrate a comprehensive understanding of the work, and they persuade readers to accept the writer's interpretation and evaluation of a work of literature by providing evidence.

The New Standards expectations for responding to literature in writing center on this more formal, school-based genre. In the world outside of school, this genre is realized in published reviews of books, poetry, short stories, or other texts. Reviews are judged for the writer's ability to craft effective and defensible commentary—a coherent analysis that is supported by evidence.

The New Standards expectations for student writers in the response to literature genre require that student writers provide an introduction, demonstrate an understanding of the work, advance an interpretation or evaluation, include details from the literature that support the writer's assertions, use a range of appropriate strategies, and provide closure. Supporting judgments with evidence from the text is at the heart of this genre.

Orientation and Context

There are many ways to introduce a response to a literary work, depending upon the writer's purpose, but introductions usually share some common elements. Context is typically provided, such as the subject of the literature, the identity of the author(s), and the title(s) of the work or works that will be discussed. The writer may also attempt to engage the reader's interest by suggesting a reason for the reader to want to read the literature or by using an attention-grabbing lead. Some writers articulate the main point of their response in the introduction.

Comprehension, Interpretation, and Evaluation of Literature

The core of a response is the writer's interpretation and evaluation of the literature. Successful writers of this genre make assertions about the work that focus on the important elements of the text. They demonstrate comprehension of the work and a good grasp of the significant ideas of the work or passages in the work. They advance judgments that are interpretive, analytic, evaluative, or reflective, dealing with ambiguities and complexities in the text(s). They deal with questions about motivation, causality, and implications. They typically comment on the author's use of stylistic devices and show an appreciation of the effects created. They make perceptive judgments about the literary quality of the work.

Effective writers of this genre illustrate their interpretations or evaluations of the literature (for example, evaluations of an author's craft, interpretations of a work's theme) with examples or other information about the text. It is common for writers to summarize or paraphrase the work, or relevant parts of it, but successful writers of this genre do not simply retell. They make choices about what to tell the audience and what not to tell, depending upon the points they want to make.

Writers of this genre also sometimes compare and contrast the work they are responding to with other works that they have read or with their own life experiences. They may draw analogies between events or circumstances in literature and events or circumstances in their own lives. In other words, they connect the literature to their life experiences or culture. They support their interpretations or inferences by explaining the characters' motives or the causes of events based on their understanding of people and life in general. They often use quotations to explain and support their interpretation or to illustrate aspects of the author's craft. Used appropriately, quotations add to the credibility of the writer's conclusions.

Evidence

When students write a formal response to literature, they make a judgment about something they have read or have heard read to them. This judgment can be evaluative ("I liked it because…") or it can be interpretive ("I think the author is saying…"). Successful writers of this genre develop credible arguments to support their judgments. Significantly, this genre requires students to go back into the text to support their evaluation or interpretation. Although reader-response approaches stress the value of individual and unique encounters with text, reader-response theorists do not advocate the idea that every reading of a text is as good as any other. Louise Rosenblatt (1968) says that we must challenge students to be disciplined in the way they work with texts by (1) showing what in the text justifies their response and (2) making clear the criteria or standards of evaluation that they are using.

Because the deep structure of response to literature is argument, usually more than one assertion is put forward, and each is supported by evidence. Individual assertions add weight to the argument and relate back to the writer's overall interpretation or evaluation of the text. In order to make sense of the writer's interpretation or evaluation of a text, the audience needs adequate evidence—examples, details, quotations—along with explanations and reasons. Successful writers of this genre support their interpretations, inferences, and conclusions by referring to the text, other works, other authors, or to personal knowledge. They move beyond purely associative or emotional connections between the literature and their own experience (text-to-self connections) to explain how the connections they write about support their interpretations and evaluations. They convince the reader through logic and with evidence that is both sufficient and relevant. They typically use connecting words associated with reasoning (because, so, the first reason). If they are comparing works, they make accurate and perceptive observations of the similarities and differences between the works, and they support their observations by referring to the texts.

Successful writers of this genre express their feelings and reactions, but they do not overly rely on appeals to emotions or overstate their case. Although young children may often exaggerate or make sweeping generalizations, as they mature, their arguments are more often based on logic and reasoning. Successful writers of this genre do not make hasty generalizations marked by words like "all," "ever," "always," and "never." They qualify their claims, using words like "most," "many," "usually," and "seldom," when such words would be more accurate, and they support their opinions with evidence.

Closure

Although a response to literature may not always have a formal conclusion, writers typically provide some sort of closure, such as a summing up of the writer's perspective on the work. Writers of this genre often leave the reader with a fresh insight, a quotation, or some other memorable impression.

Response to Literature in First Grade

Students' understanding of the features of the response to literature genre varies widely in first grade. Less advanced students may not provide an introduction, or even the title of the text. They may start right in with a retelling ("Wilfred is not old yed but Wilfred asc Nacy [Nancy] wut is memerys [what are memories]"). Some may use the book title to introduce the topic ("The West Texas Chili Monster"). Some will make only scant, or very general, reference to the content of the text, and their own ideas may not be clearly or coherently articulated. They may make loose associations with experiences in their own lives ("The story reminds me of when I ate chili and it burned my tongue.")

Students who meet the standard for writing a response to literature at first grade will typically introduce the topic, either through the title or in a brief introduction ("Things we learned about Mem Fox's books."). They have much more control and fluency, and they provide more background information for the reader than do students in kindergarten. If they are responding to an informational text, they provide a general, and sometimes detailed, overview of the topic. If they are writing about a story, their retellings are fairly complete. They use simple evaluative expressions to state opinions about the text ("You should read this book because it was funny.") or parts of the text ("My favorite part was when Eric follwed her to her secret hideing place and when she learned how to read because the little girl was the author of the book Patricia Placco."). They also give reasons for their reactions ("I like the storei Wilfrid becose a little boy helps a old lady get her memry back..."). They make simple comparisons to events or people in their own lives. They are able to compare two books by the same author and discuss several books on the same theme. They present plausible interpretations of the books they read, and they refer to the work or parts of it when presenting or defending a claim.

Response to Literature Rubrics Elements

	5 Exceeds Standard*	4 Meets Standard
Orientation and Context	• May rely on the title of the work to introduce the topic.	• May rely on the title of the work to introduce the topic.
Comprehension, Interpretation, and Evaluation of Literature	• Demonstrates a literal understanding of the work. • Uses simple evaluative expressions to state reactions to the work or parts of the work (e.g., "Mem Fox writes funny storys.").	• Demonstrates a literal understanding of the work. • Uses simple evaluative expressions to state reactions to the work or parts of the work (e.g., "Mem Fox writes funny storys.").
Evidence	• Provides a relatively detailed retelling of narrative text (or a summary of an informational text). • Provides detail to support reaction, interpretation, or evaluation (e.g., "She writes some books that are sad. Like Sophie when her grandpa dided [died]."). • May quote fragments of dialogue when retelling.	• Provides a relatively detailed retelling of narrative text (or a summary of an informational text). • Provides detail to support reaction, interpretation, or evaluation (e.g., "She writes some books that are sad. Like Sophie when her grandpa dided [died]."). • May quote fragments of dialogue when retelling.
Closure	• Typically provides closure.	• Typically provides closure.

	3 Needs Revision	2 Needs Instruction	1 Needs Substantial Support
Orientation and Context	• May rely on the title of the work to introduce the topic.	• May rely on the title of the work to introduce the topic.	• May not provide any form of introduction, even the title of the work.
Comprehension, Interpretation, and Evaluation of Literature	• Demonstrates a literal understanding of parts of the work. • Uses simple evaluative expressions to state reactions to the work or parts of the work.	• May demonstrate a literal understanding of parts of the work. • Uses simple evaluative expressions to state reactions to the work or parts of the work.	• May demonstrate some superficial understanding of parts of the work. • May use simple evaluative expressions to state reactions to the work.
Evidence	• Provides some sense of the narrative (or what the topic is if responding to informational text), but may not articulate it completely. • May refer to specific content of the work. • May quote fragments of dialogue when retelling.	• Provides some sense of the narrative (or what the topic is if responding to informational text), but may not articulate it completely. • May refer, but only generally, to the content of the work. • May use a simple list structure (e.g., "I like…") to organize reactions to parts of the work. • Typically does not include quotations.	• Does not articulate a story line if a retelling of a narrative is attempted. • Typically makes only scant or general reference to the content of the work. • Typically does not include quotations.
Closure	• May provide closure.	• May simply stop.	• Typically does not provide closure.

*The criteria that define score points 5 and 4 are identical. This is intentional. What distinguishes a 5 from a 4 is not the presence or absence of a particular element or strategy. Rather, it is the overall quality of execution and the level of language the writer employs. Writers of score point 5 papers bring something to the next that may not be provided by instruction—a deep understanding or passion for the topic and the genre.

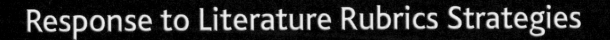

Response to Literature Rubrics Strategies

	5 Exceeds Standard*	4 Meets Standard
Compare/ Contrast	• If discussing two or more works, describes incidental similarities between them. • May loosely associate events in the work with events in own life.	• If discussing two or more works, describes incidental similarities between them. • May loosely associate events in the work with events in own life.
Other	• May refer to literary techniques or concepts (e.g., "The characters are Mama, Inez, Lorenzo, Isabel, Alfones, Alma, Baby and The Chili Monster.").	• May refer to literary techniques or concepts (e.g., "The characters are Mama, Inez, Lorenzo, Isabel, Alfones, Alma, Baby and The Chili Monster.").

	3 Needs Revision	2 Needs Instruction	1 Needs Substantial Support
Compare/ Contrast	• If discussing two or more works, may describe incidental similarities between them. • May loosely associate events in the work with events in own life.	• If more than one work is mentioned, typically does not compare events or text features; may simply mention favorite parts. • May loosely associate events in the work with events in own life.	• If more than one work is mentioned, typically does not compare events or text features; may simply mention favorite parts. • Typically does not refer to events in own life.
Other	• Typically does not refer to literary techniques or concepts (e.g., characters).	• Typically does not refer to literary techniques or concepts (e.g., characters).	• Typically does not refer to literary techniques or concepts (e.g., characters).

*The criteria that define score points 5 and 4 are identical. This is intentional. What distinguishes a 5 from a 4 is not the presence or absence of a particular element or strategy. Rather, it is the overall quality of execution and the level of language the writer employs. Writers of score point 5 papers bring something to the next that may not be provided by instruction—a deep understanding or passion for the topic and the genre.

Score Point 5

Response to Literature Student Work and Commentary: "Things We Learned About Mem Fox's books"

> Things We Learned About
> Mem Fox's books
> Mem Fox Likes to write childrens
> book. She loves to write about animals
> old people and young people. She also
> writes funny book for exsampel Night
> Noises because she had a speach
> buble that said wheres the toilet. She
> writes some books that are sad.
> Like Sophie when her grandpa dided.
> In most of her books she
> teches us stuf not to do
> and things that it's

This piece discusses the lessons the writer has learned from reading several of Mem Fox's books, including *Night Noises, Tough Boris, Whoever You Are, Sophie,* and *Time for Bed*. The piece is unusual because first graders typically write about only one text in a response to literature. The writer makes statements about Fox's books and provides examples from the books to support those statements. This piece exceeds the standard for response to literature in first grade.

The piece begins with a statement about Mem Fox ("Mem Fox likes to write children's book.").

The writer makes assertions about Mem Fox's books, and she provides details from the books to support her statements about them ("She writes some books that are sad. Like Sophie when her grandpa dided."; "In most of her books she teches us stuf not to do and things that it's alright to do Like in Tough Boris she teaches us that it's alright for boys to cry.").

The writer quotes a fragment of dialogue in her discussion of *Night Noises* ("she had a speach buble that said wheres the toilet").

The piece closes with a discussion of the theme in *Time for Bed* ("I think the theam is everyone has to go to bed some time."). The writer's use of the term "theme," and her ability to provide an example of a theme, demonstrate her understanding of a literary concept.

Score Point 5 *continued*

alright to do Like in Tough Boris she teaches us that it's alright for boys to cry. In the book Whoever you are it dosen't matter if your black or white you can still be friends. Mem Fox must care about animals if she writes about them.

In the book Night Noises I wonder why Mem Fox put 3 pictures on one page? In the book Time forBed I think the

theam is everyone has to go to bed some time.

Score Point 5 continued

Assessment Summary: "Things We Learned About Mem Fox's books"

ELEMENTS		
	Exceeds Standard	**Commentary**
Orientation and Context	• May rely on the title of the work to introduce the topic.	The piece begins with a statement about Mem Fox ("Mem Fox likes to write children's book.").
Comprehension, Interpretation, and Evaluation of Literature	• Demonstrates a literal understanding of the work. • Uses simple evaluative expressions to state reactions to the work or parts of the work (e.g., "Mem Fox writes funny storys.").	The writer makes assertions about Mem Fox's books ("She writes some books that are sad.").
Evidence	• Provides a relatively detailed retelling of narrative text (or a summary of an informational text). • Provides detail to support reaction, interpretation, or evaluation (e.g., "She writes some books that are sad. Like Sophie when her grandpa dided [died]."). • May quote fragments of dialogue when retelling.	The writer provides details from the books to support her statements about them ("She writes some books that are sad. Like Sophie when her grandpa dided."; "In most of her books she teches us stuf not to do and things that it's alright to do Like in Tough Boris she teaches us that it's alright for boys to cry."). The writer quotes a fragment of dialogue in her discussion of *Night Noises* ("she had a speach buble that said wheres the toilet").
Closure	• Typically provides closure.	The piece closes with a discussion of the theme in *Time for Bed* ("I think the theam is everyone has to go to bed some time.").

STRATEGIES		
	Exceeds Standard	**Commentary**
Compare/ Contrast	• If discussing two or more works, describes incidental similarities between them. • May loosely associate events in the work with events in own life.	The piece describes similarities between Mem Fox's books.
Other	• May refer to literary techniques or concepts (e.g., "The characters are Mama, Inez, Lorenzo, Isabel, Alfones, Alma, Baby and The Chili Monster.").	The writer's use of the term "theme," and her ability to provide an example of a theme, demonstrate her understanding of a literary concept.

Note: The commentary highlights the elements and strategies in the student paper, focusing on how well the paper addresses the totality of the elements and strategies rather than on whether each is included.

Score Point 4

Response to Literature Student Work and Commentary: "Ther once was a boy..."

> Ther ~~oneeonce~~ was a boy and he lived next to som old pepel. He liked eveyone ther. But the one he rily likes is Nancy. He helped one of the old pepel to get her memry back. She liked eveything in the box. ~~sh~~ She felt eveything. Then she got her memry.

This response to Mem Fox's *Wilfrid Gordon McDonald Partridge* was written in two sessions. The writer provides a retelling of the story and states her opinion about the book. This piece meets the standard for response to literature in first grade.

The writer introduces the topic to readers in the piece's title.

The writer's retelling of the book demonstrates her understanding of it ("He helped one of the old pepel to get her memry back." and "a littel boy helps a old lady get her memry back...").

The writer uses simple evaluative statements to state her reactions to the book, and she provides details to support her evaluations ("I like it for a nather reesane and this is why. The boy is verey nice to the pepel and has good ideas and he dos not be mean.").

The writer's evaluation of the text closes the piece.

The writer does not make connections with her own life or refer to literary techniques.

Score Point 4 *continued*

I like the storei
Wilfrid becose a littel
boy helps a old lady
get her memry back
and I like it becose
for a nather reesane
and this is why. The
boy is verey nice.
to the pepel and has
good ideas and he
dos not be mean.

Score Point 4 *continued*

Assessment Summary: "Ther once was a boy…"

ELEMENTS		
	Meets Standard	**Commentary**
Orientation and Context	• May rely on the title of the work to introduce the topic.	The writer introduces the topic to readers in the piece's title.
Comprehension, Interpretation, and Evaluation of Literature	• Demonstrates a literal understanding of the work. • Uses simple evaluative expressions to state reactions to the work or parts of the work (e.g., "Mem Fox writes funny storys.").	The writer's retelling of the book demonstrates her understanding of it ("He helped one of the old pepel to get her memry back." and "a littel boy helps a old lady get her memry back…"). The writer uses simple evaluative statements to state her reactions to the book ("I like it for a nather reesane…").
Evidence	• Provides a relatively detailed retelling of narrative text (or a summary of an informational text). • Provides detail to support reaction, interpretation, or evaluation (e.g., "She writes some books that are sad. Like Sophie when her grandpa dided [died]."). • May quote fragments of dialogue when retelling.	See commentary above. The writer uses simple evaluative statements to state her reactions to the book, and she provides details to support her evaluations ("I like it for a nather reesane and this is why. The boy is verey nice to the pepel and has good ideas and he dos not be mean.").
Closure	• Typically provides closure.	The writer's evaluation of the text closes the piece.
STRATEGIES		
	Meets Standard	**Commentary**
Compare/ Contrast	• If discussing two or more works, describes incidental similarities between them. • May loosely associate events in the work with events in own life.	
Other	• May refer to literary techniques or concepts (e.g., "The characters are Mama, Inez, Lorenzo, Isabel, Alfones, Alma, Baby and The Chili Monster.").	
Note: The commentary highlights the elements and strategies in the student paper, focusing on how well the paper addresses the totality of the elements and strategies rather than on whether each is included.		

Score Point 3

Response to Literature Student Work and Commentary: "KoAlA Lou is my favorite Book"

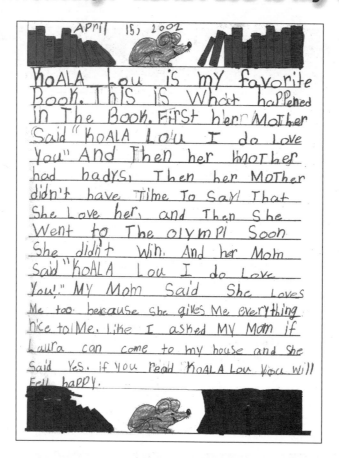

In this response to literature, the writer provides a general retelling of Mem Fox's *Koala Lou*, and she makes connections between the book and her own life. This response to literature approaches, but does not meet, the standard for first grade.

The writer begins by making a simple evaluative statement about the book ("KoALA Lou is my favorite Book.").

The majority of the response is a retelling of the book that provides a sense of the book for readers ("FirSt her MoTher Said 'KoALA Lou I do Love You' And Then her moTher had badys [babies], Then her MoTher didn't have Time to Say That She Love her..."). In Mem Fox's book, Koala Lou feels that her mother does not tell Koala Lou she loves her enough after Koala Lou's siblings are born. Koala Lou enters the Bush Olympics in hopes of gaining her mother's attention. At the end of the book, Koala Lou's mother reminds her, "Koala Lou, I do love you."

The writer does not provide details or reasons to explain why *Koala Lou* is her favorite book.

The writer quotes fragments of dialogue in her piece ("And her Mom Said 'KoALA Lou I do Love You!'").

The piece closes with an address to the reader ("if you read KoALA Lou You will Fell happy.").

The writer associates events in the text with events in her own life ("My Mom Said She Love Me too because she gives Me everything nice to Me.").

Score Point 3 continued

Assessment Summary: "KoAlA Lou is my favorite Book"

ELEMENTS		
	Needs Revision	**Commentary**
Orientation and Context	• May rely on the title of the work to introduce the topic.	The writer begins by making a simple evaluative statement about the book ("KoALA Lou is my favorite Book.").
Comprehension, Interpretation, and Evaluation of Literature	• Demonstrates a literal understanding of parts of the work. • Uses simple evaluative expressions to state reactions to the work or parts of the work.	The writer's retelling demonstrates her understanding of the book. See commentary below. The writer makes a simple evaluative statement ("KoALA Lou is my favorite Book.").
Evidence	• Provides some sense of the narrative (or what the topic is if responding to informational text), but may not articulate it completely. • May refer to specific content of the work. • May quote fragments of dialogue when retelling.	The majority of the response is a retelling of the book that provides a sense of the book for readers ("FirSt her MoTher Said 'KoALA Lou I do Love You' And Then her moTher had badys [babies], Then her MoTher didn't have Time to Say That She Love her..."). In Mem Fox's book, Koala Lou feels that her mother does not tell Koala Lou she loves her enough after Koala Lou's siblings are born. Koala Lou enters the Bush Olympics in hopes of gaining her mother's attention. At the end of the book, Koala Lou's mother reminds her, "Koala Lou, I do love you." The writer does not provide details or reasons to explain why *Koala Lou* is her favorite book. The writer quotes fragments of dialogue in her piece ("And her Mom Said 'KoALA Lou I do Love You!'").
Closure	• May provide closure.	The piece closes with an address to the reader ("if you read KoALA Lou You will Fell happy.").
STRATEGIES		
	Needs Revision	**Commentary**
Compare/ Contrast	• If discussing two or more works, may describe incidental similarities between them. • May loosely associate events in the work with events in own life.	The writer associates events in the text with events in her own life ("My Mom Said She Love Me too because she gives Me everything nice to Me.").
Other	• Typically does not refer to literary techniques or concepts (e.g., characters).	

Note: The commentary highlights the elements and strategies in the student paper, focusing on how well the paper addresses the totality of the elements and strategies rather than on whether each is included.

Possible Conference Topics

The writer will benefit from a conference to discuss providing details to support her reactions to or evaluations of the work.

Score Point 2

Response to Literature Student Work and Commentary: "The name of the book i read…"

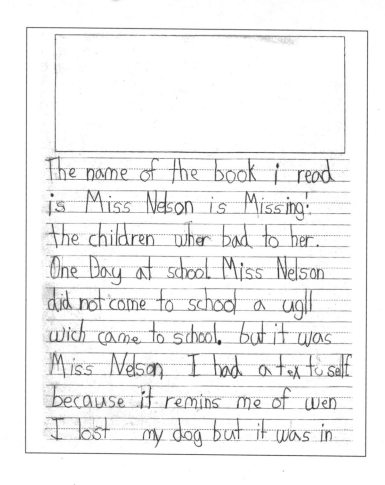

The name of the book i read
is Miss Nelson is Missing:
the children wher bad to her.
One Day at school Miss Nelson
did not come to school a ugll
wich came to school. but it was
Miss Nelson I had a tex to self
because it remins me of wen
I lost my dog but it was in

In this response to literature, the writer discusses *Miss Nelson Is Missing!* by Harry G. Allard. The piece provides some sense of the narrative, but the writer refers to the work only generally, and he does not provide details to support his reaction to it. This piece does not meet the standard for a response to literature in first grade.

The writer uses the title of the book to introduce the topic in the first sentence ("The name of the book i read is Miss Nelson is Missing!").

The writer's retelling of the book demonstrates a literal understanding of parts of the work ("the children wher bad to her. One Day at school. Miss Nelson did not come to school a ugll wich came to school. but it was Miss Nelson."). In Allard's book, Miss Nelson disguises herself as Viola Swamp, a mean substitute teacher, to make her misbehaving students appreciate her. The class is so glad for Miss Nelson's return that they behave. The writer's retelling does not communicate the reasons for Miss Nelson's disguise.

The writer closes the book by recommending it to readers ("You chud [should] read this Book because the children did not no wher she was."). The reason he provides does not really support his recommendation.

The writer loosely associates events in his life with events in the book ("I had a tex to self because it remins me of wen I lost my dog but it was in my grog [garage].").

Score Point 2 *continued*

my grog. you chud read this Book
because the children did not
no wher she was.

Assessment Summary: "The name of the book i read..."

ELEMENTS		
	Needs Instruction	**Commentary**
Orientation and Context	• May rely on the title of the work to introduce the topic.	The writer uses the title of the book to introduce the topic in the first sentence ("The name of the book i read is Miss Nelson is Missing!").
Comprehension, Interpretation, and Evaluation of Literature	• May demonstrate a literal understanding of parts of the work. • Uses simple evaluative expressions to state reactions to the work or parts of the work.	The writer's retelling of the book demonstrates a literal understanding of parts of the work ("the children wher bad to her. One Day at school. Miss Nelson did not come to school a ugll wich came to school. but it was Miss Nelson.").
Evidence	• Provides some sense of the narrative (or what the topic is if responding to informational text), but may not articulate it completely. • May refer, but only generally, to the content of the work. • May use a simple list structure (e.g., "I like...") to organize reactions to parts of the work. • Typically does not include quotations.	In Allard's book, Miss Nelson disguises herself as Viola Swamp, a mean substitute teacher, to make her misbehaving students appreciate her. The class is so glad for Miss Nelson's return that they behave. The writer's retelling does not communicate the reasons for Miss Nelson's disguise.
Closure	• May simply stop.	The writer closes the book by recommending it to readers ("You chud [should] read this Book because the children did not no wher she was."). The reason he provides does not really support his recommendation.
STRATEGIES		
	Needs Instruction	**Commentary**
Compare/ Contrast	• If more than one work is mentioned, typically does not compare events or text features; may simply mention favorite parts. • May loosely associate events in the work with events in own life.	The writer loosely associates events in his life with events in the book ("I had a tex to self because it remins me of wen I lost my dog but it was in my grog [garage].").
Other	• Typically does not refer to literary techniques or concepts (e.g., characters).	

Note: The commentary highlights the elements and strategies in the student paper, focusing on how well the paper addresses the totality of the elements and strategies rather than on whether each is included.

Next Steps in Instruction

This writer will benefit from instruction on providing a retelling of the book that demonstrates an understanding of it and providing details from the book to support the writer's reaction to it.

Score Point 1

Response to Literature Student Work and Commentary: "Wilfred"

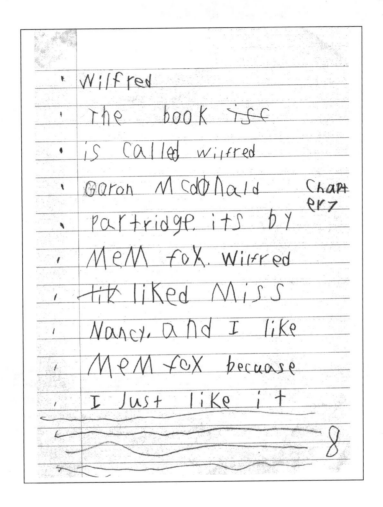

Wilfred

The book isc
is called wilfred
Goron McdoNald   Chapt
                                 er7
Partridge. its by
MeM fox. Wilfred
tit liked Miss
Nancy. and I like
MeM fox becuase
I Just like it

This response to Mem Fox's *Wilfrid Gordon McDonald Partridge* is very brief and associative ("I like Mem fox becuase I Just like it"). The writer clearly struggles for something to say about the book. Because this book is well beyond what we expect first graders to be able to read by themselves, it could be that there are gaps in comprehension because the writer's attention drifted as the book was being read aloud.

The writer introduces the piece by naming the book in the first sentence ("The book is called Wilfred Goron Mcdonald Partridge.").

The piece includes only very scant and general reference to the content of the book ("Wilfred liked Miss Nancy.").

There is no attempt to articulate a story line. In Mem Fox's book, Wilfrid helps his elderly friend Miss Nancy remember some of the incidents of her childhood, but the writer does not recount those events for readers.

Although the piece is brief, it lacks coherence ("Wilfred liked Miss Nancy. and I like Mem fox becuase I Just like it.").

There is no closure.

Score Point 1 *continued*

Assessment Summary: "Wilfred"

ELEMENTS		
	Needs Substantial Support	**Commentary**
Orientation and Context	• May not provide any form of introduction, even the title of the work.	The writer introduces the piece by naming the book in the first sentence ("The book is called Wilfred Goron Mcdonald Partridge.").
Comprehension, Interpretation and Evaluation of Literature	• May demonstrate some superficial understanding of parts of the work. • May use simple evaluative expressions to state reactions to the work.	The writer's references to the book are so scant that it is difficult to determine how much he understands. The piece includes a simple evaluative statement ("I like Mem fox...").
Evidence	• Does not articulate a story line if a retelling of a narrative is attempted. • Typically makes only scant or general reference to the content of the work. • Typically does not include quotations.	There is no attempt to articulate a story line. In Mem Fox's book, Wilfrid helps his elderly friend Miss Nancy remember some of the incidents of her childhood, but the writer does not recount those events for readers. The piece includes only very scant and general reference to the content of the book ("Wilfred liked Miss Nancy."). Although the piece is brief, it lacks coherence ("Wilfred liked Miss Nancy. and I like Mem fox becuase I Just like it.").
Closure	• Typically does not provide closure.	The piece simply stops.
STRATEGIES		
	Needs Substantial Support	**Commentary**
Compare/ Contrast	• If more than one work is mentioned, typically does not compare events or text features; may simply mention favorite parts. • Typically does not refer to events in own life.	
Other	• Typically does not refer to literary techniques or concepts (e.g., characters).	
Note: The commentary highlights the elements and strategies in the student paper, focusing on how well the paper addresses the totality of the elements and strategies rather than on whether each is included.		

Roadmap for Development

The writer needs time to develop the confidence and stamina necessary for producing longer pieces. The writer may also need a fuller understanding of the book—perhaps some oral discussion—before attempting a written response.

References

Black, P., & Wiliam, D. (1998). Inside the black box: Raising standards through classroom assessment. *Phi Delta Kappan, 80*(2), 139–149.

Bruner, J. (1985). Narrative and paradigmatic modes of thought. In E. Eisner (Ed.), *Learning and teaching the ways of knowing* (pp. 97–115). Chicago: University of Chicago Press.

Cooper, C.R. (1999). What we know about genres, and how it can help us assign and evaluate writing. In C.R. Cooper & L. Odell (Eds.), *Evaluating writing: The role of teachers' knowledge about text, learning, and culture* (pp. 23–52). Urbana, IL: National Council of Teachers of English.

Derewianka, B. (1990). *Exploring how texts work*. Newtown, Australia: Primary English Teaching Association.

Hillocks, G., Jr. (1984). What works in teaching composition: A meta-analysis of experimental treatment studies. *American Journal of Education, 93*(1), 133–170.

Rosenblatt, L. (1968). A way of happening. *Educational Record, 49*, 339–346.